THE SMILE OF BLAZING WINGS
and Other Plays

The Smile of Blazing Wings
and Other Plays

By
Sid Sondergard

Exposition Press   *Hicksville, New York*

First Edition

© 1978 by Sid Sondergard

All rights reserved, including the right of reproduction in whole or in part, in any form or by any means, electronic or mechanical, including photocopying, recording, or by any information storage and retrieval system. These plays are subject to royalty. All rights, including professional, amateur, motion picture, radio, television, recitation, public reading, and any other methods of reproduction, are strictly reserved. All inquiries concerning professional and amateur productions should be addressed to S. T. Logan, 741 Pippin Circle, Office 17, Wichita, Kansas 67203.

No part of this book may be reproduced without permission in writing from the publisher. Book inquiries should be addressed to Exposition Press, Inc., 900 South Oyster Bay Road, Hicksville, N.Y. 11801

ISBN: 0-682-49023-7

Printed in the United States of America

To my wife, Jackie, who tarries on

Contents

The Smile of Blazing Wings   9

When the Fires Burn in Kansas   33

National Park   77

THE SMILE
OF BLAZING WINGS

Characters

ARTHUR ALTERA, the father
AGNES ALTERA, the mother
ANNIE ALTERA, the daughter
HARMON ALTERA, the son
ANNOUNCER, the voice

Scene: The stage is a tri-level house: dining/living room at the base, HARMON's room above it, and the attic, uppermost.

Spotlight comes on and pans quickly over the contents of the dining/living room. There is a table at whose head is seated ARTHUR, *facing the audience. He is dressed normally except for a long black scarf of some elastic material, which is wrapped horizontally around his head, completely hiding his nose and mouth. The spotlight is turned off after a complete sweep, and the stage lights come on.* ARTHUR *is looking expectantly off stage right, and* AGNES *enters from stage left. She is dressed normally except for the elbow-length black gloves she is wearing. They are pulled on loosely, with about an inch too much slack left in each finger. She begins arranging plates and silverware on the table.*

ARTHUR: *(Each time he speaks,* ARTHUR *pulls the elastic scarf out from the bottom, not enough for the audience to see his nose or mouth, just enough to be heard when he speaks loudly)* Where's Annie and Harmon?

AGNES: Annie's in her room. She'll be down in a minute. *(Continues arranging tableware. Her long gloves cause her to knock over glasses, and she has to reset them several times)* I have no idea where Harmon is. He came home right after school and then left just before I went shopping.

ARTHUR: Oh. You get anything?

AGNES: *(Stiffens and puts her hands behind her back)* Get anything?

ARTHUR: Yeah. Anything exciting happen?

AGNES: Exciting?

ARTHUR: While out shopping. Anything exciting happen?

AGNES: Oh. No, dear. Nothing. *(Continues arranging tableware)* Nothing exciting at all. *(Pause)* How was your day?

ARTHUR: Rotten, until I left the office.
AGNES: And then what happened?
ARTHUR: What do you mean by that?
AGNES: What happened after you left the office?
ARTHUR: Who said anything happened? *(He begins fiddling around with his scarf)*
AGNES: You said your day was rotten, until you left the office.
ARTHUR: That's right; it was. So what?
AGNES: So what happened to change it?
ARTHUR: Oh. I . . . came home.

They look at each other silently for a moment.

ANNIE *enters from stage right. She is dressed normally except for the entirely black pair of sunglasses she wears. She feels props as she moves, similar to the technique of a blind person in unfamiliar territory.*

ANNIE: Hi, mom. Daddy?
ARTHUR: Yes, dear. I'm here.
ANNIE: Thought so. Need any help, mom?
AGNES: No, dear. Just have a seat.

AGNES *and* ANNIE *sit in two chairs on the right side of the table.*

ARTHUR: So, what've you been up to, Annie girl?
ANNIE: *(Sinks slightly into her chair)* Up to, daddy? I haven't done anything.
ARTHUR: Nothing? Don't they teach you anything at that school?
ANNIE: Oh, at school? *(Adjusting her sunglasses)* Just the usual.

The three stare from one to another in silence for a few moments.

AGNES: Well, Harmon should be along just any time.
ARTHUR: He's certainly taking his time.
AGNES: What?

The Smile of Blazing Wings

ARTHUR: I say, he's certainly taking his time.
AGNES: Oh.
ARTHUR: Let's go ahead and eat.
ANNIE: We need to say grace.
ARTHUR: Grace?
AGNES: Arthur, we do need it.
ARTHUR: Okay, okay.

The three bow their heads.

Bless this food, O Lord. Keep us—*(Pause; resumes gravely)* Keep us safe from the evils of the world—
AGNES: God, yes.
ARTHUR: —guard the innocent—
ANNIE: Please guard the innocent.
ARTHUR: —and watch over the unfortunate. Amen. *(Raises his head and starts eating)*
AGNES: *(Looking up with a worried expression)* Annie, was there any word on the little Ferris boy today?
ANNIE: He's still in Emergency at the hospital. Multiple stab wounds—
ARTHUR: Yes, yes, we know. Please remember we're trying to eat.
ANNIE: Our teacher said his family was taking him out of school.
AGNES: It's a tragedy the police can't stop the criminal that— that could *do* such a thing to a little boy.
ANNIE: Oh, I'm sure the person can't help hersel—*(Puts her hand over her mouth.* AGNES *gives her a sharp look)* himself. Can't help himself.
ARTHUR: That's probably true, *(Finishes chewing)* so until they *do* catch him, no member of this family will be allowed out after dark.
AGNES: That's a good idea.

HARMON, *walking swiftly, enters from stage right. He is wearing a long black trench coat that hangs down below his knees.*

HARMON: Am I included in that curfew? *(He sits in the remaining chair, smiling)*
ARTHUR: You betcha, young man. Say, *(Pointing to HARMON)* you figure it's going to rain in here, son?
HARMON: Any second, dad. *(To AGNES, quick follow-up)* Mom, you afraid you're going to tarnish the plastic tumblers?
AGNES: Sure I am. *(To ANNIE, quick follow-up)* Tell me, is the sun too bright for you here in the dining room, dear?
ANNIE: Yep. *(To ARTHUR, quick follow-up)* Have you got a cold, daddy, or foot-and-nose disease?

Family laughs heartily as though a very funny joke has been told. The laughter quickly degenerates, however, and becomes a nervous cackling, an empty gesture.

ARTHUR *gets up from his chair, walks downstage to a television set facing the dining table. He turns it on and returns to his seat. The fading laughter of the others subsides as the voice of the* ANNOUNCER *comes on.*

ANNOUNCER: . . . before going on to the weather, we have just received word of a second case of child molesting in this community within one week. Police are presently on the scene at Haven Hill Park, where the incident occurred at approximately five-thirty P.M. . . .
AGNES: My God, that was only forty-five minutes ago!

While AGNES *is making this speech,* HARMON *rushes to the television and turns it off.* ANNIE *begins a similar movement, but stops when she sees that* HARMON *will get there before she does.*

ARTHUR: *(Sits with his hands over his eyes while the* ANNOUNCER *is speaking. When he hears the television click off, he yells to* HARMON*)* Hey, what're you doing? I haven't heard the weather report.
HARMON: It makes me sick. This whole business makes me sick. *(Clutches his stomach)* Molesting little kids. It's sick. Sick.

The Smile of Blazing Wings 15

> (*Puts one hand to his forehead, the other grabs the front of his coat, as though to make sure it is closed*)

ANNIE: (*Putting her hands over her dark glasses*) Sick. Sick.
AGNES: (*Hiding her hands behind her back*) Sick; it really is.
ARTHUR: (*Adjusting his scarf*) Sick is what it is.
HARMON: I—I think I'll go up to my room.

HARMON *exits.*

ARTHUR: (*Shakes his head solemnly. Pause*) There's something wrong with this family, Agnes. I've failed you all.
AGNES: Don't say that, Arthur. Harmon will be all right. He's just—sensitive. (*Bites her lip, looks at* ANNIE *suspiciously, not sure just how much of the conversation she is paying attention to. She leans over, waves her hand in front of* ANNIE's *dark glasses, without receiving any reaction. She settles back in her chair and continues*) After all, he *is* a teenager. (*Rises; to* ARTHUR) Can I get you anything for dessert, dear?
ARTHUR: Oh, a small dish of seed would be nice.

> AGNES *carries dishes off stage left.* ANNIE *is staring across the table at* ARTHUR. *He shifts in his chair while she remains motionless.* AGNES *returns with a small saucer and a box labeled "Birdseed." She gathers up the remaining dishes, dropping a few, and again exits stage left.*

ANNIE: (*Still motionless. She watches* ARTHUR *as he stuffs handfuls of birdseed up under the scarf. With tone of sincere concern*) Daddy, do you really like birdseed?
ARTHUR: (*Sputters, spitting out a mouthful of seed, mutters without lifting scarf*) Mmmmmmph, mmmmmmph mmmmmmph.
ANNIE: What?
ARTHUR: (*Lifting scarf*) I said, of course I don't.
ANNIE: You don't like it?
ARTHUR: Hate it. Hate the stuff.
ANNIE: Then why do you eat it?

ARTHUR: Because, young lady, it's good for my bil—*(Drops the scarf down momentarily, then lifts it back up)* My build. Good for my build. *(No reaction from ANNIE)* Besides, we wouldn't want it to go stale, now, would we?

ARTHUR shoves a handful of seed up under the scarf. ANNIE sits motionless. Blackout.

Lights come on in HARMON's room. There are two windows in the room, one located in the center of the room and one near the left extreme. Just right of the window in the center is a full-length mirror. There is a bed and a desk near the right wall of the room. HARMON, still wearing the long black coat, is pacing back and forth.

HARMON: What is happening? What is *happening?* The whole world is going crazy. *(Stops in front of mirror. Turning his back to the audience, he stands in front of the mirror and opens his coat. Audience cannot see the reflection)* God! I can't be seeing this. It can't really be there. I must be going crazy. *(Closes coat, fastens it, resumes his nervous pacing)* But—what if I'm not? Who can I trust?

Someone knocks on the door to his room. ANNIE opens it and walks in.

ANNIE: *(Still wearing dark glasses)* You feeling okay?
HARMON: *(Shakes his head "no")* How's Billy Ferris? Was he at school yet today?
ANNIE: Come on, are you kidding? In a couple of months, maybe.

Uneasy silence.

Besides, his parents won't let him come back. They're taking him out of school.

The Smile of Blazing Wings

HARMON: *(Sits down on the bed and buries his head in his hands)* Good. *(Softer)* Good.

ANNIE: All I know is he didn't get hurt at school. Taking him out of school isn't going to help anything.

HARMON *is silent.*

Say, didja hear that they broke in on the show after the news and said there's a ten o'clock curfew now?

HARMON: A city curfew?

ANNIE: Yeah. Daddy turned the T.V. back on, and they broke in saying there's a curfew, until they catch the weirdo, wherever she—he! . . . *(Flushes; in quieter tone)* Wherever he may be.

HARMON: *(Looks away and then begins a shooing motion with his hands)* Hey, Annie, I've got a lot of homework to do. I guess I better get started. Thanks for coming up.

ANNIE: I thought you'd feel better, knowing about the curfew.

HARMON: I do. Thanks.

ANNIE: Okay, okay. *(Starts to leave)* Don't let this get you down, Harm'. I'm sure the person responsible for all this doesn't mean to hurt anyone. *(Pleading)* I know they don't mean to hurt anyone.

ANNIE *turns and exits, closing the door behind her.* HARMON *goes to the window at the left extreme of his room. He eases it open and stares outside. After a few moments, he carefully climbs out. Shortly after he has exited,* AGNES *and* ANNIE *enter the room from the door, stage right.*

AGNES: Harmon? Harmon, honey? Where are you?

ANNIE: He was here just a minute ago.

AGNES: *(Sits down on bed)* He's taking these tragedies in the park much too seriously. It's as if he felt responsible. But that's unfair. *(Bows her head slightly)* After all, *he* isn't responsible.

ANNIE: No, it sure isn't *his* fault. *(Starts toward the door)* I'll be in the living room.

ANNIE closes the door behind her. Pause; she reopens door, turns off the light switch, and again closes door. There is just enough light in the room to see AGNES as she rises and goes to the window.

AGNES: Fly away, Agnes; fly, fly away. *(She crosses her arms, then uncrosses them and stares at the long black gloves)* They can't very well blame someone else; now, can they? *(Pulls a book from the desk. She turns it to read the binding)* Noble Birds of America. How about the noble eagle, queen of the skies? Fly away, Agnes; fly away.

In singsong manner.

> "In all the world there's not a laugh
> Upon the tongues of kings;
> And madness is the sadness in
> The smile of blazing wings."

AGNES remains at the window, flapping her arms slowly up and down. She makes a couple of wild yells, similar to the sound of a large bird of prey. Blackout.

Lights come on in living/dining room. ARTHUR and ANNIE are in chairs in front of the television. Their speeches and the ANNOUNCER's overlap.

ANNOUNCER: ... detectives at the scene of today's incident have turned up several interesting clues. Several burnt matches—
ANNIE: Not matches!
ARTHUR: Sssssshhhh! Can't hear.
ANNOUNCER: —and bits of fluff that appeared to be duck feathers—
ARTHUR: Duck feathers!

The Smile of Blazing Wings

ANNIE: Sssssshhhh! Can't hear.
ANNOUNCER: —were found near the site of where a small boy was attacked by an animal—
ARTHUR and ANNIE: An animal!
ANNOUNCER: —like assailant—
ARTHUR: *(Greatly relieved)* Oh, an animal-like assailant.
ANNOUNCER: —was repeatedly stabbed in the stomach and abdomen, and slashed across the face. For further updates, stay tuned to this channel.
ARTHUR: *(Walks over to turn off television)* That sounds pretty crazy to me. Sounds like the work of a real sickie.
ANNIE: Uh-huh.
ARTHUR: And those things they found at the park? Weird.
ANNIE: *(Uneasy)* Yeah . . . burnt matches?
ARTHUR: *(Also uneasy)* And duck feathers?

ARTHUR *begins fumbling with his scarf, tightening it.* ANNIE *rises from her chair and walks over to the wall where the light switch is located. She turns out the lights and the room is just light enough to be able to see both* ANNIE *and* ARTHUR.

Hey, Annie! Why'd you turn the light off? I can't see.
ANNIE: Um, to, um, to save on the electric bills, daddy.
ARTHUR: *(Lights up a cigar and puffs on it, so the glowing red end can be seen by the audience)* I swear to God this family gets nuttier all the time. *(Puffs on cigar)* Crap, I'm still hungry. I think I'll get a little seed to munch.

ARTHUR *lays cigar down on ashtray with glowing end facing audience and exits stage right.*

ANNIE *for a moment fumbles with her dark glasses. Finally she takes them off, though reluctantly. She looks around her in the dark, until she spots the glowing red end of the cigar. She stands bolt upright and runs to the ashtray. She finds* ARTHUR's *matches and quickly pockets them. Staring at the glowing cigar, she puts her arms straight out at her sides and begins running around the ashtray in circles. She sighs and moans audibly in* pleasure. *The moans become louder, reaching ecstatic proportions.*

ARTHUR *reenters from stage right and gropes in the dark.*

ARTHUR: What's going on? Annie? Is that you running around the room?

ANNIE *breaks out of the circle, runs back to her chair and hurriedly puts her dark glasses back on.*

ANNIE: Running, daddy?
ARTHUR: *(Gropes for light switch and turns it on)* You heard me. *(Stuffs a handful of birdseed up under his scarf, talks with his mouth full)* Whuh yuh wunnig awoun' i' thuh woom?
ANNIE: Just stretching my legs, daddy.

ANNIE *turns toward the television and stares at it, as though it is turned on.* ARTHUR *sets a saucer of seed on the arm of his chair and sits down. As he does so, his arm bumps the saucer and knocks it onto the floor. He looks at* ANNIE, *who is still facing the television and not watching him. Deciding she is not going to turn, he bends down and begins pecking at the seed on the floor. He has a hard time of it, as he must lift his scarf to do so, without revealing his mouth or nose to the audience. At this point, he unconsciously begins making soft quacking noises. Being engrossed in his activities, he does not notice when* ANNIE *turns toward him and studies his action intently.*

ANNIE: Daddy?
ARTHUR: *(Jumps to his feet. Looks all around him, trying to appear nonchalant)* Something the matter, honey?
ANNIE: Daddy, what were you just doing?
ARTHUR: Doing? Why, uh, *(Picks up his cigar, begins puffing madly, though it is now extinguished)* why, just enjoying this swell cigar, darling.
ANNIE: On the floor?
ARTHUR: The floor? Why, I—*(Desperate)* I was picking up some ash that fell off the cigar.

The Smile of Blazing Wings

ANNIE: With your mouth?
ARTHUR: Annie, I think it's time for you to do your homework.
ANNIE: Why were you picking up ashes with your mouth, daddy?
ARTHUR: To your room. Now.
ANNIE: Does quacking help you pick up the ashes with your mouth, daddy?
ARTHUR: *(Explodes, pointing off stage left)* Your room! Now!

ANNIE exits stage left. Satisfied she has gone, ARTHUR again bends down and resumes his pecking. ANNIE returns, sticks her head in the room, reaches for the light switch and turns off the lights. Blackout.

Lights come on in HARMON's room just enough to see AGNES sitting on top of the desk, her legs drawn up under her like a bird in a nest. Short pause; the window is eased open from the outside by HARMON. He crawls in through the window with a pile of books under his arm. He closes the window and fumbles around in the dark, till he finds the light switch. When he turns it on, AGNES screams, and HARMON drops his books.

AGNES: *(Putting one gloved hand to her chest)* Oh, Harmon! You nearly scared me to death!
HARMON: You! What about me? This is my room, isn't it? *(Short pause, while he stares at her)* Mom, er, what are you doing on my desk?
AGNES: *(Looks down at her legs, sheepishly unfolds them and dangles them over the edge of the desk)* Oh, I was just, uh, doing my yoga exercises, dear.
HARMON: In the dark?
AGNES: *(Emphatic)* Oh, yes! It does wonders for my concentration. *(Changing the subject)* By the way, young man, where have you been?
HARMON: Over at Tommy's.
AGNES: Doing what?
HARMON: *(Looking down at the books on the floor)* Just borrowing some books for a report.

AGNES: *(Also looking at the books)* You borrowed library books from Tommy?

HARMON: Uh, sure, we're both doing the report.

AGNES: Didn't your father tell you not to leave the house?

HARMON: Oh, mom, yeah, but . . . but the report's due tomorrow.

AGNES: Well, at any rate, *(Pointing to the window)* wouldn't the front door have been an easier way to go?

HARMON: *(Still looking at the books)* Sure, but—*(Bends down and picks up the books)* I thought I'd get a little extra exercise. It's not easy climbing up and down the tree out there, let me tell you! Especially when you've got an armload of books!

AGNES: If you've got so much studying to do, I guess I'd better leave.

HARMON: Thanks, mom.

AGNES: Awfully quiet up here.

HARMON: Maybe a little music *would* be nice. *(Points to the radio on his desk)* Would you turn the radio on for me, mom?

AGNES: Oh . . . of course, dear.

AGNES reaches for the radio knob and tries to turn it on, but fumbles each time she tries, due to the loosely flopping fingers of the gloves she is wearing. HARMON has seated himself at the desk and does not see her futile struggle, as he is concentrating on one of his books.

HARMON: *(Without looking up)* The turn-on knob's on the right side, mom.

AGNES: I know, dear.

HARMON: *(Pause, while AGNES continues to struggle)* What's the matter, isn't it plugged in?

AGNES does not answer; instead, she backs up about three steps and swoops at the radio. HARMON looks up as she is about halfway into her approach. She stops abruptly and smiles sheepishly.

AGNES: There must be something wrong with the knob.

The Smile of Blazing Wings

HARMON *shakes his head, stands up, and turns the radio on.*

ANNOUNCER: —Later reports have indicated that the slash marks on the victim's face were induced by clawlike devices—

AGNES: *(Rushes at radio and yanks on the cord connecting it to the wall outlet. She crosses her arms, with the black-gloved hands under her armpits)* Now it's claws! Can't we get away from those awful reports!

HARMON: Never mind the music, mom. I really don't need it.

AGNES: After all, you'll be able to concentrate much better without all that distraction.

HARMON: Sure, mom.

AGNES: *(Starts to leave through door; turns around)* Don't study too hard, dear. *(Closes door behind her)*

HARMON: *(Sits down at desk and opens one of the books. Begins reading aloud, slowly)* Okay, here's something. "The Honeybee: family Hymenoptera, one of the social insects, a—" *(Gasps)* Family what! *(Retraces line with his finger)* "The Honeybee: family Hymenoptera." Hymenoptera? *(Jumps up from his chair and runs to the mirror. Stands talking to his reflection. Repeats slowly)* Hymen-optera. Hymen . . . optera. *(Puts his hand to his head)* Harmon Altera. Hymen-optera. Harmon Altera is a Hymenoptera. Holy Jeez! *(Runs back to the desk)* Where's my pen? Where is it? Oh, God, what's happening? *(Shoves some papers around on his desk, frenzied. Suddenly he picks up a book and stops)* What the—*(Turns the book over. The cover is ripped open and cloth hangs in shreds. Pause)* It looks like someone took a razor blade to my book. *(Turns the book sideways and reads aloud what is written on its spine)* Noble Birds of America. *(Jumps up and runs to the mirror; flailing his arms)* What next, bee-boy, what next?

Blackout.

Lights come on in attic. ANNIE *is sitting cross-legged on the floor, lighting one match after the other and holding it till it burns out.*

ANNIE: How could they have found burnt matches? I didn't even have any matches today. It must be these glasses. I've got to get darker glasses. Ouch! *(She tosses a match that has burnt almost to her fingers. She quickly strikes another)* Maybe I should wear a scarf like daddy's over my eyes? It's always so tempting—so tempting to . . . *(Pause. She stares intently at the flame as it burns down. Slowly, she removes her dark glasses with one hand while holding the match with the other)* It's—so *beautiful*. So *perfect*. Like gold. Ouch! *(Again she tosses the match because it has burnt so low. She sits for a moment in darkness)* This is the last match. How can I stand to see it go out? The last match. Last one for now. They burn so quickly. Oh, I hope this one burns slow. I want it to last forever. *(She lights the match. As it ignites, she begins moaning with pleasure)*

AGNES: *(From offstage)* Annie, is that you in the attic?

ANNIE *blows out the match. Blackout.*

Lights come on in the dining/living room. ARTHUR *is sitting alone at the dinner table. Next to him is the box of birdseed.*

ARTHUR: *(Talks in between handfuls of seed)* Nuthouse. That's what it is. Me, the head squirrel—I mean, duck. Well, hell, what am I supposed to do? Go see a shrink? What'll he tell me? "Mr. Altera, your problem is very simple. As a child you hated your father and loved your mother. Now you despise your son and misunderstand your wife and daughter." I'll say, "Sure doc, so how come I've got a bill where my nose used to be?" *(Munching seed)* This seed's great stuff, once you get used to it. I guess even ducks have to acquire a taste for it. *(Pause)* So what am I going to do with this nutty family of mine? You'd think *they*—

AGNES *enters along with* ANNIE, *who is holding a Monopoly game.*

AGNES: Game time, game time.
ANNIE: This'll be so much fun. I haven't beat daddy in a *long* time.

She starts setting up the board. Blackout.

Lights come on in HARMON's *room. He is sitting dejectedly on the edge of his bed.*

HARMON: So what do I do? Tell them about it? Sure. Simple. *(Stands up, motions with his hands)* "Dad, a funny thing happened today. I finally looked up what my problem is. I've become a bee. Like some honey?" *(Sits down on the bed again)* If I had any guts, I'd—*(Slowly stands up and walks over to his desk)* If I had any guts . . . *(Picks up a pair of large scissors. Slowly he opens and closes them, then closes them and sits back down on the bed)* I guess there's one way to find out how good these scissors are.

Blackout.

Lights come on in dining/living room. ARTHUR, AGNES *and* ANNIE *are seated around the dining table, with the Monopoly board set between them.*

ANNIE: *(Moving her game token)* Oh, good. Around "Go" again for two hundred more dollars.
ARTHUR: Hey, that's my token. The top hat.
ANNIE: *(Withdrawing the token. Lifting her dark glasses ever so slightly)* Sorry, it looked like the thimble to me.
AGNES: There, dear, this one is yours. *(Reaches for a token and knocks off token, houses, motels, etc., with her gloves)*
ARTHUR: Hey, watch it! You're knocking everything off. What's wrong with you people?
AGNES and ANNIE: What?
ARTHUR: *(Stretching his scarf much more than usual)* I said, what's wrong with you people?
AGNES: Well, I'm just upset about Harmon.

ARTHUR: What am I supposed to do? You want me to go up and talk with him?
AGNES: No, you don't have to. I'm just concerned. *(Pause, while she surveys the Monopoly board)* A mother's concern.
ANNIE: C'mon, mom, it's your move.

AGNES sits surveying board. Pause. ANNIE sighs, rises, and walks over to the television. When she turns it on, the sound of Indian war whoops is heard.

ARTHUR: Not a Western, Annie.

No response.

Hey, turn it down.
AGNES: *(Staring offstage, looking worried)* I'm going to see what he's up to. *(Rises)* He wasn't made for worry. It wears on him.

AGNES exits stage right.

ARTHUR: Bunch of fruit-loops, that's what this family is.

ANNIE scoots a chair up to the television so she is sitting with her face right up to the screen. ARTHUR puts his fingers in his ears, grimaces, then pulls out a loose end of his scarf that has been tucked into his shirt and wraps it under his chin and over his head, to cover his ears.

AGNES comes running in from stage right, with HARMON by the arm.

AGNES: *(Breathless)* I—found—
ARTHUR: *(Unwrapping his scarf from his ears)* Huh?
AGNES: I—found—Harmon—up—
ARTHUR: *(To HARMON, who has his head bowed, looking at his feet)* Son, have you gotten more of those magazines—?
HARMON: Oh, no, dad, I know those aren't good for me.
AGNES: *(Waving her hands)* No, he wasn't *reading* anything— not like he tried to make me believe he was.

ARTHUR: *(Shaking his head slowly)* Son, son, I told you that that sort of thing can only lead to blindness and insanity.
HARMON: *(Almost crying)* Gee, dad, I was only—
ANNIE: What did you *do*, Harmon?
ARTHUR: Hush, Annie. What did you *do*, Harmon?
AGNES: He was using scissors!

The others look at her.

ARTHUR: So what's wrong with using scissors?
AGNES: *(HARMON again bows his head)* He was using them to cut the crotch out of his jeans!
ARTHUR: While he had them on?
ANNIE: Oh, that's sick.
HARMON: *(Pleading)* I had to, dad.
ARTHUR: *(Crosses his arms; patiently)* Okay, son. Explain it to me.
HARMON: *(Shrugging)* Well, dad, I really don't know where to begin. Something—something's happened to me.
ARTHUR: *(Putting his hands slowly over his eyes)* Oh, God, I knew it'd come to something like this. I was afraid it'd rub off.
AGNES: *(Putting her hands over her eyes)* Why didn't I just leave? Why have I done this to my own family?
ANNIE: *(She has joined the scene and also covers her eyes)* Don't feel bad, mom, dad. I couldn't help what I did.
HARMON: *(Surveys the scene, amazed)* Hey, *(Yells)* what's wrong with you people?

They all look up at him.

I'm the one with the problem, here. I don't believe any of you are growing—*(Pause; swallows)*—are growing stingers.
ANNIE, AGNES and ARTHUR: Stingers!
HARMON: *(Looking down at his coat)* Why else would I be wearing this stupid coat?
ARTHUR: *(Shaking his head)* You're a sick boy, Harmon. Your mother was right about you. *(Points at the coat)* Open your coat.

HARMON: Do what!
ARTHUR: *(Stern)* You heard me, son. Open that coat.
HARMON: *(Crying)* No! Dad, please, don't. They'll put me in a cage.
ARTHUR: Son, they'll put you in a padded cell if you don't.
HARMON: *(Puts his arms around himself)* Don't make me open it.
ANNIE: Daddy, maybe—
ARTHUR: I know what's best for you. Open it, son.
HARMON: But, dad—
ARTHUR: Now! Don't argue with—
HARMON: *(Interrupting)* Besides, what—what about you? Why don't you *(Pointing)* take off that scarf!
AGNES: *(Shocked)* Harmon Altera!
ARTHUR: Making fun of real problems won't help you with your make-believe ones, son.
AGNES: *(Standing with a finger to her chin, thoughtfully)* On the other hand, now that something's been said, he's right, dear. You're always having to pull that silly scarf up and yell so we can understand you.
ARTHUR: Oh yeah? Well, Mrs. Gloves, *(Pointing)* while we're exposing eccentricities, let's see you take those off!
ANNIE: Don't, daddy; she doesn't cause any trouble with them.
ARTHUR: *(Now furious)* And for that matter, what about you, little blind girl? I haven't seen your eyes for weeks!
HARMON: *(Waving his hands)* Please, stop it, all of you. Don't fight because of me. I'll just leave.
ARTHUR: No you don't, young man.

HARMON *has turned away and begun to leave.* ARTHUR *grabs him and spins him around so they are face to face. After doing so, he puts his hands on the lapels of* HARMON's *coat and rips it open.* HARMON *screams and shuts his eyes tightly, as* ARTHUR *tears the coat off of him and throws it to the floor.* ARTHUR *turns to* AGNES.

Next! Step right up!

ARTHUR, *in a frenzy of sadistic pleasure, grabs* AGNES *by the hands, and, while she screams, "No! You can't!" he yanks her gloves off. She also screams and shuts her eyes.* ARTHUR *turns to* ANNIE.

Here I am, the Seeing-Eye Dog!

ANNIE has been frozen to the spot, but now starts to run while ARTHUR jumps and knocks her down. Pinning her to the floor, he tears off her dark glasses and throws them across the room. She also screams and puts her hands over her eyes. While ARTHUR has been bending over her, however, HARMON has crept up behind him and now proceeds to grab an end of ARTHUR's scarf and run. As he does so, it pulls off. ARTHUR is dumbstruck.

Wha—what—what the hell have you done?

Slowly, everyone looks at one another, moving like scanners from face to face. A deep gutteral buzz begins issuing from HARMON's *throat.* AGNES *begins flapping her arms slightly.* ANNIE *puts her arms slowly out at her sides and begins walking in a wide circle around the room.* ARTHUR *himself slowly assumes a squatting position on the floor.*
    HARMON *begins buzzing very loudly and starts chasing around the room, butting his rear into objects like the wall, etc., as though he were "stinging" them.*
    AGNES *begins yelling, "Scree! Scree!" She flaps her arms madly and swoops from place to place. Periodically, she takes swipes at objects with her fingernails, knocking things over.*
    ANNIE *is now running quickly in circles around the light fixture in the center of the room. She makes a loud, ecstatic moaning sound as she runs.*
    ARTHUR *is doing something like an awkward waddle in a crouching position. He yells, "Quack! Quack!" as he does so.*
    The television during all this time has been issuing war whoops and gunfire from the movie Western that has been showing. After a brief period, the ANNOUNCER's *voice breaks in.*

ANNOUNCER: We interrupt this program to announce a third in a series of child molesting incidents. The latest incident occurred at eight-thirty-five P.M., approximately fifteen minutes ago . . .

The family members stop all motion and sound, listening intently.

. . . in Winthrop Memorial Park.

ARTHUR *slowly stands up.* AGNES *stands still.* ANNIE's *arms drop to her sides.* HARMON *stops running into things.*

Witnesses at the scene described the assailant as an elderly man, five foot, ten inches, one hundred forty-five pounds, with silver-white hair and a small, trimmed moustache. Police have already taken a suspect matching this description into custody. Anyone possessing information relating to this or other incidents is asked to . . .

Family members start looking from one to another.

. . . call the Police Department, extension five twenty-nine, and ask for Lieutenant Baker.

As ANNOUNCER's *voice fades, war whoops and gunfire replace it.* ARTHUR *scratches his head, strokes his cheek, and slowly walks back to the chair he occupied at the table during the opening of the play. Slowly, the others join him, until all of them are seated as they were during the dinner scene.*

ARTHUR: *(Clears his throat)* Er, I, uh—
ANNIE: C'mon, daddy. Do you want Marvin Gardens or not?
AGNES: Now, don't be pushy, darling. Daddy will decide for himself.
HARMON: Who's the banker here? Where's my money?
AGNES: Be patient. I'll count out your money for you.

ANNIE: What's the matter, daddy? Do you want it or not?
AGNES: Yes, do you want it?
HARMON: Come on, answer us. Do you want it or not?
ARTHUR: *(Pushes at an imaginary scarf, then realizes it is no longer there and sheepishly bows his head. He speaks very softly)* No, I don't want it.
HARMON: *(Along with* AGNES *and* ANNIE, *breaks into great laughter)* He doesn't want it!
ANNIE: He doesn't want it?
AGNES: He doesn't want it!
HARMON, AGNES and ANNIE: So he's gonna get it!

Laughing, they jump up from their chairs and drag ARTHUR, *in his chair, into the center of the room. They then grab hands and begin skipping, chanting in a circle around* ARTHUR.

AGNES: "In all the world there's not a laugh—"
ANNIE: "Upon the tongues of kings—"
HARMON: "And madness is the sadness in—"
HARMON, AGNES and ANNIE: "The smile of blazing wings!"

ARTHUR'S *head is bowed. He sits motionless in the chair as* ANNIE *again flies around the light in a circle,* AGNES *begins flapping her arms around the room, and* HARMON *begins running at things with his rear end. This goes on for almost a minute, before* ARTHUR *buries his face in his hands. Blackout.*

There is almost thirty seconds' pause before the single spotlight, as in the beginning, comes on and begins slowly panning the stage. It finally comes to rest on ARTHUR, *sitting motionless in the chair, his face buried in his hands. The other family members are gone. Blackout.*

Curtain.

WHEN THE FIRES BURN IN KANSAS

Characters

WILLIAM C. QUANTRILL
"BLOODY" BILL ANDERSON
GEORGE TODD
FRANK JAMES
JESSE JAMES
COLE YOUNGER
ANDY BLUNT
SECRETARY OF WAR JAMES A. SEDDON
GENERAL LOUIS T. WIGFALL
CAPTAIN ALBERT PEABODY
MOSE
GUERILLAS

SCENE ONE

JESSE *is seated on a Wells-Fargo-like strongbox at the farthest point downstage and to the right. A spotlight is turned on, drifts along the stage and passes over him. It is quickly adjusted and comes to rest on him.*

JESSE: 'Lo there. I don't know you, an' don't 'magine you know me or rec'nize my face. That's gonna change.

Spotlight starts to drift away.

Hold it. I'm talkin'. Down here, son *(Points up at spotlight, and it readjusts to shine on him)* I'm s'posed to be here. Yeah, y'all may not rec'nize the face, but I'll bet the name'll ring a few bells. Jesse James. Yep, I'm *the* Jesse James. So what am I doin' here? Well, it has to do with my special line of work. Y'all remember me 'cause of a few bank an' railroad jobs me an' Frank an' the boys pulled after the Civil War days. Suffice it to say, right now I've got some words to tell 'bout the man who taught me my trade, a schoolteacher-turned-bushwhacker named Bill Quantrill. Sounds kinda familiar, you say? Let me tell you, it's a name they'll never forget in Lawrence, Kansas. They won't forget the day Bill Quantrill an' his guerilras rode into town under their black flag an' leveled almost ever'thing that stood. Quantrill an' his boys were prob'ly the most cunning an' bloodthirsty bunch of riders the West ever saw. I should know. After all, I rode with 'em. Not right at first, 'course, 'cause I was a lot younger'n my brother Frank when he an' the others took Quantrill's oath . . .

The stage is dark except for the spotlight, which now shifts to QUANTRILL, *who is standing slightly upstage and to the left of where* JESSE *is sitting. As throughout the play,* QUANTRILL *wears a red shirt and Confederate breeches. He faces half away from the audience.*

QUANTRILL:
>Today, by joining together
>With me, you become more than
>Men; you are no longer
>Accountable to laws, lawyers, or
>Law officers, for
>Today you join with me under the
>Black flag of the Confederacy,
>Under the black flag of war.
>The oath you take here today will
>Change you hereafter.
>So be it.

Stage becomes slightly lighter as ANDERSON, TODD, FRANK, YOUNGER, *and* BLUNT *form a file upstage from* QUANTRILL. *They repeat each of the following lines after* QUANTRILL *recites it.*

>In the name of God and Devil,
>One to punish, the other to reward,
>And by the powers of light and darkness,
>Good and Evil,
>Here, under the black arch of heaven's avenging symbol,
>I pledge and consecrate my heart,
>My brain, my body, and my limbs,
>And I swear by all the powers of hell and heaven
>To devote my life to obedience to my superiors;

Slowly, while the others repeat after QUANTRILL, *more* GUERILLAS *begin filing in behind* ANDERSON *and the rest of the front line. The voices repeating the oath grow in volume, until it seems that a whole army must be standing together on the dimly lit stage.*

That no danger or peril
Shall deter me from executing their orders;
That I will exert every possible means in my power
For the extermination of Federals,
Jayhawkers, and their abettors;
That, in fighting those whose serpent trail
Has winnowed the fair fields
Of our allies and sympathizers,
I will show no mercy,
But strike with an avenging arm,
So long as breath remains.
    I further pledge my heart,
My brain, my body, and my limbs,
Never to betray a comrade;
That I will submit to all the tortures
Cunning mankind can conflict,
And suffer the most horrible death,
Rather than reveal a single secret
Of this organization,
Or a single word of this, my oath.
    I further pledge my heart,
My brain, my body, and my limbs,
Never to forsake a comrade
When there is hope,
Even at the risk of great peril,
Of saving him from falling
Into the hands of our enemies;
That I will sustain Quantrill's guerillas
With my might and defend them with my blood,
And, if need be,
Die for them.
In every extremity I will never withhold my aid,
Nor abandon the cause
With which I now cast my fortunes,
My honor, and my life.
Before violating a single clause
Or implied pledge of this obligation,

I will pray an avenging God and an unmerciful devil
To tear out my heart and roast it over flames of sulphur;
That my head may be split open
And my brains scattered over the earth;
That my body be ripped up
And my bowels torn out and fed to carrion birds;
That each of my limbs be broken with stones
And then cut off by inches,
That they may be fed to the foulest birds of the air;
And lastly,
May my soul be given into torment
That it may be submerged in melted metal
And be stiffened by the fumes of hell,
And may this punishment
Be meted out to me through all eternity,
In the name of God and the Devil.
Amen.*

All lights except for the spotlight on QUANTRILL *are extinguished. The other* GUERILLAS *are no longer visible.* QUANTRILL *turns to face the audience.*

Today, death gains powerful allies
And life suffers a bitter defeat;
Barbarians all,
A death met in battle is
Life complete.

---

*This oath is faithful to the original, as recited by J. Frank Dalton, one of Quantrill's men, who died in 1951.

SCENE TWO

Spotlight is turned on JESSE. *His position is the same as before.*

JESSE: Besides havin' a flair for bein' dramatic, Bill Quantrill demanded respect. By God, he got it, too. Titles an' rank were real import'nt to him. He'd been made a Cap'n through somethin' called the Partisan Ranger Act, without even bein' a reg'lar in the Confederate Army. That wasn't enough, though. Bill pictured himself as a Colonel, an' he wanted the boys to call him "Colonel" Quantrill. Decidin' it was time to make the title official, Bill got himself an appointment to see the Sec'try of War, Mr. James A. Seddon . . .

Lights come up on stage as the spotlight is extinguished. Scene is a meeting room with a desk, behind which is seated SEDDON. WIGFALL *sits to his right, in a chair adjacent to the desk.* QUANTRILL *is joined by* BLUNT.

SEDDON:
    You place me in an awkward position, Captain Quantrill.
    You are asking me to give you
    Justification for raids, ambushes,
    Surprise attacks.

QUANTRILL:
    War is hard, Mr. Secretary; war
    Gives birth to precedents that are far
    Contrary to peacetime aims.
    Is the design of war to be
    Victorious or generous? Are we
    Soldiers, or are we
    Artists who are expected to

Create an acceptable tapestry that is
Successful, though neither
Too hostile nor
Too unconventional?
A good leader is indeed an
Artist, but his skill is not
Measured by how he applies his paints,
Rather by how he inspires his men.
You object to raids, ambushes, and
Surprise attacks. Do not
Forget that
General Washington often—

WIGFALL:
Enough lecturing. We are not
Your schoolchildren, Quantrill. This
Is the office of the Secretary of
War, not a classroom. You are speaking to
Adults.

QUANTRILL: (*Ignoring* WIGFALL)
As I was saying, Mr. Secretary,
General Washington often drilled his
Men in the surprise attack. Would you
Object to the methods on which this
Country's freedom was founded? What
I am asking is simple enough for
You to grant: the
Confidence
Of the Confederacy.

WIGFALL:
The *protection* of the Confederacy, you mean.

BLUNT:
We don't need your protection.

QUANTRILL:
Surely
You know what my forces can mean. We represent
Victory in Kansas; we can, and have defeated
Everything the

When the Fires Burn in Kansas

    Abolitionists send against us. The Missouri-Kansas
    Border War is hopeless without my raiders to
    Support Confederate movement.

SEDDON:
    Appreciating your position to us, Captain,
    Is one thing. But
    What you ask is not possible. A commission.
    You ask me for a Colonel's commission.
    It is true that the feats of you and
    Your men have already earned you a
    Captain's commission. Yet you are not a
    Regular in our army, and, as for your
    Men, they are strictly
    Renegade. To grant you a
    Colonel's commission would be like
    Giving a jailer a gold key to
    Release his most murderous inmates.

QUANTRILL:
    I will not apologize for the bravery and
    Uncompromising valor of my men.

WIGFALL:
    Valor, he says. So his pack of murderers are
    Virtuous murderers.

QUANTRILL:
    It is true that my men and I are not
    Regular soldiers in any sense. There
    Lies our strength.
    These are men with nothing to lose, all
    Glory to gain—desperate. They fight with all their
    Spirit and do not comprehend what it means
    To lose, to die while retreating. They are brave men.
    With thirty of these handpicked men, I can defeat
    What would require of you a hundred.

WIGFALL:
    He boasts!
    He begs!
    What else can he do?

BLUNT:
> Beat hell out of you.

QUANTRILL:
> You can see my men aren't regular soldiers.

WIGFALL:
> Indeed not! Regular soldiers understand the meaning of
> Discipline and respect the rank of their
> Superiors. Regular soldiers are kept in line
> By their officers, not allowed to rob and pillage
> After a victory. Regular soldiers also take
> Prisoners. Somehow, Quantrill, your prisoners
> Never make it into custody. You don't command
> Soldiers. Your men are
> Thieves, drunks,
> Criminals of every
> Variety. They're from the
> Same stock as you, Quantrill,
> Barbarians!

BLUNT:
> You'd think so if you fought us.

QUANTRILL: *(Crosses over to face WIGFALL, who remains sitting)*
> Barbarians, is it! Coming from a
> Fighting man, that sounds like a
> Cry of
> Surrender! A weak cry, at that. How
> Dare you take that tone of
> Judgment when you speak of my men. I wouldn't
> Trade one of them for fifty of you, you
> Pompous toad. You aren't even man enough to command the
> Horses my men ride. Looking at you, it seems to me
> You could use a strong dose of
> Barbarism. What kind of General
> Do you call yourself?

BLUNT:
> General-ly useless.

When the Fires Burn in Kansas

QUANTRILL:
>Barbarians! The word is synonymous with
>War; there can be no
>Distinction between the two.

>*Steps back and faces* SEDDON.

>Mr. Secretary of War, is this typical
>Of your advice concerning the future of the
>Confederacy? The war has begun, sir;
>Please don't damn the warriors. Surely
>This isn't what you want, a
>Gentleman's war, to be fought with
>Rules and
>Manners, like some blasted game of
>Horseshoes?

>*SEDDON does not reply, turns his head away.*

>You ask the impossible, Secretary Seddon; the
>Conqueror does not succeed without violence, and
>Battles are not won
>With kind words. Sitting
>Here in Richmond, you don't see what my men and
>I know too well: if Missouri falls, it becomes
>The domino that topples all else . . . Tennessee,
>Kentucky, they'll all fall. The destruction of
>Kansas is the torch that will ignite the
>Confederacy. All I ask of you is a
>Title,
>Under which to rally my men.

SEDDON:
>So you ask, Captain Quantrill.

>*He bows his head.*

>Heaven help the Kansans;
>I deny your request.

QUANTRILL:
>   I see.
>   A civilized war for you, Mr. Secretary?
>   Nothing *too* unorthodox for you.
>   Forget that I ever
>   Came here. Forget my request. Forget
>   My presence and that of my men; you will
>   Hear of us
>   Soon enough. I formally withdraw my request,
>   Sir, for what has been alleged here is
>   No less than the
>   Truth.
>   I am indeed a
>   Barbarian; I fight to win.

> QUANTRILL *pauses, staring at* WIGFALL *and* SEDDON.

>   And I never surrender.

> QUANTRILL *and* BLUNT *turn to leave.*

>   Wait.

QUANTRILL *turns back, reaches into his shirt, and pulls out a large black rectangle of cloth. He throws it at* SEDDON's *feet.*

>   There it is, Mr. Secretary. Now you've
>   Seen the barbarian's
>   Commission.
>   A Colonel? You refuse to
>   Grant me a mere title. When the
>   Fires burn in Kansas, thanks to
>   Quantrill and
>   His men, sorry will be the day you
>   Rejected him and refused to honor his

Military brilliance. Only a
Colonel. For service much more humble
Than what I will give the Confederacy,
Secretary Seddon,
Men have been made
Kings.

QUANTRILL *and* BLUNT *exit. Blackout.*

SCENE THREE

Spotlight on JESSE.

JESSE: As you can see, Bill Quantrill was one proud man. Bein' turned down by Sec'try Seddon didn't sit too well with him. Matter o' fact, it made him so mad he decided he'd give *himself* the Colonel's commission. Problem was, it took more'n a "Colonel" tacked onto his name to keep his boys in line. It got so they didn't need a reason to raid . . . they'd raid just for the sake o' raidin'. The Colonel was a leader, but it just so happened that Anderson, Todd, and others also had men followin' 'em. The showdown that had to happen was startin' to take shape . . .

Spotlight is extinguished as stage lights come on. Scene is a campfire. QUANTRILL *is seated in a central position. Surrounding him are* ANDERSON, TODD, FRANK, *and* YOUNGER.

QUANTRILL:
    Seddon acted like this should be a
    Game we're playing. He wouldn't
    Recognize a fight if it
    Busted his jaw . . . and that fat General
    Wigfall. He called us
    Barbarians, seemed to think there were
    Rules we're supposed to follow when
    Attacking. There's only one rule I
    Know of when it comes to fighting.

ANDERSON:
    Kill 'em dead.

When the Fires Burn in Kansas

QUANTRILL:
>That's the one. You know, Bill, you've
>Got quite a reputation for
>Yourself. I know where Archie Clements
>Learned his meanness. It seems the Kansas
>Redlegs have got themselves a new warning
>Cry about you. They're saying, "Quantrill
>Sometimes takes prisoners; Anderson
>Never does." I also hear you've got
>Yourself a new nickname. That right?

ANDERSON:
>Yep. They call me "Bloody" Bill Anderson.

QUANTRILL:
>"Bloody" Bill.
>Can't fault them for that.

TODD:
>How 'bout *your* new nickname?
>Is it 'ficial, now, "Colonel"?

QUANTRILL:
>Colonel William C. Quantrill now commands the
>Troops riding under the
>Black flag. Seddon couldn't very well say no
>When I told him about the care we're giving those
>Jayhawkers. Fact is, he didn't have much of
>Anything to say.

FRANK:
>I 'magine you did most of the talkin', Colonel, sir.

QUANTRILL:
>That's right, Frank. You must be rubbing off on
>Me. Of course, I haven't had your luck with
>Finding unsympathetic audiences. Only a man
>Of your talents could have managed to
>Brag about his success in battle
>When there were Federal
>Militia men standing right behind
>Him. Rare talent.

FRANK:
> Amen.

TODD:
> He's jus' lucky his ma was handy to
> Ask for his release. Some o' us ain't that
> Lucky.

YOUNGER:
> Some o' us ain't even lucky enough to
> Have mothers.

ANDERSON:
> Or fathers.

QUANTRILL:
> Anderson, I sometimes wonder if you ever had
> Either one. I think
> You were the result of a rattlesnake and a
> Vulture. The snake was coiled as the vulture
> Closed in, and when the dust and feathers stopped
> Flying, there was little Bill, all beady eyes and
> Venom.

ANDERSON:
> I'd like to spray a little venom inna some
> Kansas blood. When the hell we gonna
> Ride inna Kansas again?

QUANTRILL:
> Soon, "Bloody" Bill. Tomorrow we're going through
> Jackson County on the way to the border. It's
> Time we showed the Redlegs we mean business. I
> Want bushwhackers to be the topic of every
> Jayhawker. I want Quantrill's raiders to be
> Talked about in
> Whispers around
> Campfires. I want preachers to mention Quantrill's
> Guerillas in their prayers.
> Are your men all ready to ride?

ANDERSON:
> That's all they talk 'bout.

When the Fires Burn in Kansas

TODD:
>They're like a storm ready to break.

ANDERSON:
>My boys are tired o' waitin' for the
>Feds. They wanna go flush some out.
>They want fresh Fed scalps to hang on their
>Saddles.

QUANTRILL:
>We'll ride for the border at dawn. A few of us will
>Ride through Jackson County, the rest heading
>Straight for the line. We'll all meet up
>There before entering Kansas. Tell your men to
>Get some sleep.

All except QUANTRILL *begin to leave.*

>Cole? I'd like a word with you.

The others exit, leaving QUANTRILL *and* YOUNGER.

>Not much talk coming from Cole
>Younger this evening. Something
>Bothering you?

YOUNGER:
>It's Anderson. He went crazy while you
>Were gone. He an' his boys raided twice without
>Leavin' the state, s'posedly burnin' the
>Farms of antislavers an' Abolitionists,
>But that's just excuses. He wants blood,
>Colonel. He deserves the
>Nickname. He just doesn't know when to
>Stop. Worse'n that, there's
>More o' the men sayin' they'd follow
>Him in a second if anythin'
>Happened to you.

QUANTRILL:
    Meaning what?
YOUNGER:
    Meanin' I'm concerned 'bout what's
    Gonna happen if he's with the
    Bunch that're headin'
    Straight for the border. He's
    Liable to start more trouble'n
    We can handle. If he calls an
    Attack, the men'll follow him.
QUANTRILL:
    It wouldn't be the first time that's
    Happened, and you're right about
    Anderson's ability to start trouble
    We don't need. What I want you to
    Do is tell the men in the morning that
    George Todd will be leading them to the
    Border.
YOUNGER:
    But Anderson—
QUANTRILL:
    You leave him to me. George will
    Lead the men to the border without
    Bringing every Federal within a
    Hundred miles down on their tails.
    I'll take you, Anderson, Frank James, and
    Andy Blunt with me through Jackson
    County, where we hung that spy,
    Searcy, before you joined up with us.
    We'll find a farm there to stay
    Overnight at. Next morning we ride
    To meet Todd and the rest at the border.
YOUNGER:
    Anderson'll want to start a couple o'
    Fights on the way.
QUANTRILL:
    If he's smart, he won't start them

When the Fires Burn in Kansas 51

With me. Anderson's a good man in a
Fight, but I'm in command here, and he'd
Better remember that.
Get yourself some rest now, Cole;
I'm counting on you to help me keep
An eye on "Bloody" Bill.

      YOUNGER *nods and exits.*

What kind of leader would
Bill Anderson make? He'd lead the men
Into an ambush, just as
Soon as he'd go a
Mile out of his way to avoid it.
I'll have to watch him. There's
Only room for one leader with this
Outfit. We'll see who leads when the
Fires burn around us and the
Bullets start flying
Hard and fast.

      QUANTRILL *exits. Blackout.*

SCENE FOUR

Spotlight on JESSE.

JESSE: Colonel Quantrill, as the boys started callin' him, kept an eye on ole "Bloody" Bill. Things were quiet for a while, while they rode through Jackson County, but it didn't last long. The boys stopped for the night at a farm belongin' to a fella named John Flannery . . .

Lights slowly come up on stage. Scene is a single-roomed farmhouse. QUANTRILL, YOUNGER, BLUNT, FRANK, *and* ANDERSON *are lying under blankets on the floor.*

That woulda been fine, 'cept that the Feds happened to get wind o' the news. It so happened that Gen'ral Jim Lane, who commanded all the Kansas Militia, ordered a Cap'n Peabody an' his company to hunt Quantrill's bushwhackers down. It wasn't too hard to find 'em. The trails they left were almost always the same: dust an' dead men . . .

Voices yell from offstage. The men all rise from their bedrolls, while QUANTRILL *goes to a window and peers out. Spotlight on* JESSE *is extinguished.*

QUANTRILL:
    There's trouble outside. Federal trouble.
ANDERSON:
    We'll show 'em what trouble is.
PEABODY: *(From offstage)*
    Quantrill! Captain Quantrill! This is Captain Peabody.

You and your men are surrounded. There's no way out
Except through us. Surrender and you
Will not be harmed. You will be treated as
Prisoners of war.

ANDERSON:
Like hell we will.

YOUNGER:
We can't surrender. They'd
Shoot us like coyotes.

QUANTRILL:
We need time to think.

He yells out the window.

Captain Peabody! This is Colonel Quantrill.
Give me fifteen minutes to talk
With my men. We will give you an
Answer then.

PEABODY: *(From offstage; pause)*
Fifteen minutes, then, Quantrill. No
Longer. And no tricks.

FRANK:
We can't go out the back way. They've got men
Posted there, too. We're surrounded.

QUANTRILL:
Our only chance is to charge them
From the front. We can wait until nightfall,
Hold them off and make them think we're
Running out of ammunition. Unless, of course,
You want to surrender.

YOUNGER:
We wouldn't live five minutes if we
Surrendered. They'd shoot us an' scalp us.

QUANTRILL:
We haven't a chance of outnumbering them, so
Maybe we can outsmart them.

ANDERSON:
>Outsmart 'em, hell. There's only one thing them Feds
>Unnerstand. This.

He breaks the window and fires his gun outside. There is a yell, and loud firing from outside commences.

>How's that for an answer, boys?

>*He yells out the window.*

>How's that for an answer, Cap'n?

QUANTRILL:
>That was stupid, Anderson. If we'd been
>Ready, we could've each killed a man
>With our first shots. Now they'll probably
>Charge the house.

ANDERSON:
>Words. You think words'd save us? We're gonna have to
>Fight our way out.

QUANTRILL:
>You haven't made it any easier
>For us to do that.

PEABODY: *(From offstage)*
>Give up now, Quantrill, or we'll kill
>Every last one of you.

QUANTRILL: *(Yelling out the window)*
>You'll have to shoot us if you want us at
>All, Peabody. Colonel William Quantrill
>Does not surrender.

FRANK:
>That's right. We'll give 'em a fight they'll remember.

YOUNGER:
>Colonel, look. They're lightin' torches.

QUANTRILL:
>Damn. So they mean to burn us out.

When the Fires Burn in Kansas 55

All of QUANTRILL's *men are now firing their pistols out the window intermittently.*

> A couple of you grab the pillows from the
> Bed and all the clothing you can.

BLUNT *and* FRANK *gather as per* QUANTRILL's *instructions.*

> They've lit the house. It won't hold out
> For long. Hurry with the clothes.

Some red lighting is directed onstage. BLUNT *and* FRANK *deposit a pile of clothes at* QUANTRILL's *feet.*

> Start stuffing the clothes. We're making
> Dummies out of cloth. Maybe we can also make a
> Few out of the Federals.

ANDERSON:
> That ain't gonna help us none.

QUANTRILL:
> Shoot your gun instead of your
> Mouth. Blunt, James, set the dummies up in
> Front of the windows. The last thing
> Those soldiers will expect is for us to come
> Charging right at them
> From the front door.

BLUNT *and* FRANK *set dummies near windows.*

> We'll show them that
> Bravery is the best surprise attack.
> I'll lead out, Anderson behind
> Me; Blunt, you follow him.
> James and Younger, I want one of you to
> Cover us from the rear.

YOUNGER:
> I'll go out last. Just be sure you
> Run like hell.

QUANTRILL:
> Just as soon as we get clear, split
> Up and head into the woods. If they
> Follow, we'll ambush them. Keep moving, and
> Meet in the big clearing north and east
> Of here.

ANDERSON:
> Quit talkin' an' let's move.

QUANTRILL:
> Keep firing with both hands.

The others put a pistol in each hand.

Ready, now!

QUANTRILL *slams open the door, runs offstage screaming and firing his guns, followed by* ANDERSON, BLUNT, FRANK, *and* YOUNGER. *When all have exited, there is a slight pause while the sound of gunfire fades. Blackout.*

SCENE FIVE

Spotlight on JESSE.

JESSE: You shoulda seen the looks on the faces o' those Feds when Quantrill and the boys burst outa that house, runnin' straight at 'em. The Feds were so shook that they all got away. Cole Younger did some mighty fancy shootin' from the rear that sure helped. 'Course, when the Feds saw that bright red shirt with two guns ablaze comin' right at 'em, it was all they could do to keep from turnin' an' runnin'. After meetin' up later, the boys managed to steal some horses an' made it to the border, where George Todd an' the other guerillas were waitin'. A couple o' raids later, soon after they'd escaped from Peabody's unit, Cole was restin' up in the home of a friend named Amos Blythe, when he heard 'bout a force of Feds from Independence that were comin' to get 'im. Cole relayed the warnin' to Colonel Quantrill, who decided they'd set up an ambush for the troops on the road 'tween Independence and Harrisonville, near Blue Cut. Well, they set up to spring the trap an' waited for what seemed like hours. It looked like somethin'd gone wrong, so the Colonel sent Cole to investigate. He was a few miles from Blue Cut, when he ran into ole Mose, one o' Amos Blythe's slaves . . .

Lights come up on stage as spotlight is extinguished. An old Negro runs breathlessly up to YOUNGER.

MOSE: *(Waving his arms wildly)*
Massa Younga! Massa Younga!
Lord, protec' us; oh, itz terr'ble.

YOUNGER:
>Settle down, ole fella. What's the
>Matter? Where's Amos?

MOSE:
>Massa Younga, oh, wha' dey done
>To de boy, to Massa Blythe's boy.
>Lord, hab mercy!
>Wha' dey done t'his boy.
>Dey killed de young man, killed 'im.
>Dey sho' killed 'im.

YOUNGER: *(Shaking* MOSE*)*
>Mose, hold it. Tell me what happened.
>What happened to Amos's boy?

MOSE:
>Oh, Massa Younga, de Union soljahs come
>A-ridin' into de place an' dey
>Grab Massa Blythe's boy—

YOUNGER:
>Which one of the slaves did
>They kill? Adam? Joshua?

MOSE:
>No, suh, tha's what I'se
>Tryin' to tell you. Dey didn'
>Grab one us darkies, no, suh,
>Dey grab Massa Blythe's *boy.*

YOUNGER: *(Gripping* MOSE *tightly)*
>His son?

MOSE:
>Yassuh, yassuh, dey grab de
>Pore chile an' tried make 'im
>Say where was Massa Blythe hid.

YOUNGER:
>Amos got away, didn't he? I
>Told him to hide out
>Somewhere till the troops
>Left.

MOSE:
> Yassuh, yassuh, he done lak
> You tole 'im to. He done
> Hid 'fore de troops come to
> Look fo' 'im.

YOUNGER:
> Then tell me what happened.

MOSE:
> Dey took de pore boy inna de barn
> An' says dey was gonna hang 'im
> Iff'n he didn' tell where was hid Massa Blythe.
> Well, suh, dis brave young man
> Wasn' 'bout to tell where was hid
> His ole daddy. So he runs away
> Into de house, an' grabs an ole
> Gun. Soon as he does, he runs lak
> De devil into de woods. Lordy, dem
> Soljahs seen de pore chile runnin',
> So's dey aims an' shoots 'im in
> De back. Even den, suh, dis brave chile
> Pulls de triggah twice an' kills
> Two of de soljahs befo' he dies. Den,
> Suh, while he was whisperin' a las'
> Prayer to de preshus Lord, dey
> Steps up to de boy an'
> Shoots roun' afta roun' ob bullets
> Inna his pore body. Dis was too
> Much for ole Mose. I'se been runnin'
> Ebah since. Lordy, wha's to do,
> Massa Younga?

YOUNGER:
> Mose, you get back to the farm
> And you tell Amos that those
> Soldiers are dead men. I promise
> You that. 'Fore sunset, those
> Union cowards'll be
> Rottin' meat.

Lights on stage go down, as the spotlight on JESSE *comes on.*

JESSE: Cole Younger was a decent enough, fair man, an' shootin' another man in the back was somethin' that could make his blood boil. Shootin' a boy who was tryin' to protect his ole man made Cole crazy. Well, he took a look from a rise along the road an' saw that the Union soldiers were headin' back up the road. Seems they'd taken a roundabout way to get to the Blythe place an' had gone completely aroun' Blue Cut, where the ambush was. So Cole hightailed it back to where Quantrill was waitin' with the rest . . .

Spotlight out, lights come up. QUANTRILL *is crouched near a rock as* YOUNGER *enters.*

YOUNGER:
    Colonel, they're comin'! An' we're gonna
    Pay them back for the pain they've caused
    Amos Blythe!

QUANTRILL:
    Blythe? What's happened? How'd they
    Get past us?

YOUNGER:
    They took the long way 'roun' Blue
    Cut. They got to Amos's place an'
    He was hidin'. So they grabbed his
    Son an' shot him down in
    Cold blood. With Union bullets
    In his back, the boy was
    Still fightin'. They
    Finally had to walk up to him
    An' load him with minié balls.

QUANTRILL: *(Grave)*
    A brave boy. A leader, most
    Likely. They'll pay, the Federals, for this
    Injustice. We'll serve them the same

Dessert. Pass the word about Amos's
Son. Let the rally yell be: "Remember
Young Blythe!"

QUANTRILL *levels his pistol at a point beyond the rock, cocking it very slowly, as* YOUNGER *exits.*

The lights on stage again fade as the spotlight on JESSE *comes up.*

JESSE: There were thirty Union soldiers came ridin' through Blue Cut, while the Colonel an' his men were waitin'. They'd completely forgot 'bout the Blythe boy by then, an' were whistlin' an' singin' as they rode. They were about as unsuspectin' as possible when the gunfire started from above 'em. By the time the smoke cleared, there weren't more'n two men alive. An' since they were hidden in the woods, not one o' Colonel Quantrill's men'd been hit. They'd gotten their revenge for Amos Blythe's boy.

No break between this and the following speech.

SCENE SIX

JESSE: Things started changin' after the trouble in Blue Cut. By that time, there was close to a hunnerd men ridin' with Quantrill under the black flag. There was more close calls, more raids, more killin'. His forces'd gotten so big, the Colonel had to split 'em up under some other leaders. He split into four groups: under himself, Bill Haller, Cole Younger, an' George Todd. If you think Bill Anderson was mad at not bein' chosen, you ain't seen what mad is. He was ready to tear somebody apart. Anybody. Too bad for the town of Lawrence, Kansas, he got news that one of his sisters'd been killed an' another one crippled for life in the cave-in of the Union prison where they were bein' held. He got blood fever. Along with the rest o' Quantrill's band, Anderson burned an' killed his way through Lawrence. Fathers, men of all ages, were dragged out o' their homes an' shot in the street. I'd just joined the bushwhackers, but the Colonel'd refused to let me ride to Lawrence, said I was too young. Just as well, I guess. After Lawrence, ever'thin' started goin' downhill. Cole Younger quit the Colonel's outfit an' became a reg'lar in the Confederate Army. Ever'body seemed to have got their fill of blood for a while. Ever'body, that is, 'cept for "Bloody" Bill Anderson . . .

Spotlight is extinguished as stage lights come up. Scene is just across the Kansas border. With QUANTRILL *are* BLUNT, FRANK, *and* ANDERSON.

QUANTRILL:
>Now the Unionists will know the
>Meaning of fear. If Seddon could see

The smoke rising, wouldn't he call us
Barbarians now! Lawrence will
Serve as an example of what will
Happen to all antislavers who
Dare to anger
Quantrill's guerillas.

FRANK:
Where's George Todd? He was s'posed to
Scout the area an'
Meet us back here.

QUANTRILL:
Todd will return soon. He may have
Run into a unit that we
Somehow managed to miss.

ANDERSON:
What I wanna know is, when do we
Attack again? If Lawrence was only the
Beginnin', how soon do we make a
Repeat performance?

QUANTRILL:
First, we lie
Low for a few days. There'll
Be troops on our tail before
Nightfall. If we attack
Now, they'll find us and
Corner us.

ANDERSON:
An' we'll fight till we kill 'em all.

QUANTRILL:
I haven't forgotten how your
Stupidity almost got us killed in Jackson
County. There'll be no suicide raids
As long as I'm
In command here, Anderson.

ANDERSON:
That may not be as long as
You think, Quantrill.

FRANK:
>   Christ, Bill, you'd ride us right
>   Down the Yankee's gun barrels if
>   You was leadin'.

ANDERSON:
>   One thing's sure. I wouldn't go hidin',
>   'Fraid to show my face. You
>   Can't fight from a hole in the ground, an',
>   If they corner us now, that's
>   Where we'll be.

QUANTRILL:
>   That's why we've got to keep on
>   Moving, not stay here and fight.
>   We haven't the manpower to take on the
>   Whole Union Army, Anderson. We have to
>   Cut them off a
>   Little at a time.
>   To try to do more means our death.

ANDERSON:
>   So what? You 'fraid of dyin'?

QUANTRILL *approaches, quickly pulls out his pistol, aims it at* ANDERSON's *head, and jerks it slightly, so it misses while shooting from close range.*

QUANTRILL:
>   No, I'm not. And I'm not afraid
>   To kill, either, Mr. Anderson.

> TODD *enters.*

>   Just in time, Todd. I was just
>   Drilling your friend "Bloody" Bill, here, in
>   What to expect if he ever
>   Insults me again.

ANDERSON:
>   Your time'll come, Quantrill.
>   You won't be in charge forever.

QUANTRILL:
>No, not forever.
>But by the time my command is
>Over, Anderson, you'll be
>Long dead and gone. More than likely,
>You'll be killed by your own
>Stupid foolhardiness.

ANDERSON:
>We'll see—

BLUNT: *(Interrupting)*
>Hey, Bill, let's go have some more o' that
>Lawrence whiskey we grabbed. It's
>Got a bite like a
>Rattler an' a kick like a
>Mule.

BLUNT *and* FRANK *pull* ANDERSON *along with them as they exit.* TODD *approaches* QUANTRILL.

QUANTRILL:
>I could use some of that whiskey
>Myself. Trying to reason with Anderson
>Is like trying to shoe a
>Bull. Neither one will hold still for
>More than a minute without wanting
>A fight.

TODD:
>You'd be smart to watch 'im, Colonel. He meant
>What he said 'bout you not bein' in charge
>Forever. He'd shoot you in the
>Back
>First opportunity he got.

QUANTRILL:
>There's only one other man in this
>Outfit that'd give Anderson a
>Fight over leadership. Is that
>Right?

TODD:
>Tha's right. You'd be smart to
>Keep an eye on him, too.

QUANTRILL:
>I *have* been watching you.

TODD: *(Chuckling)*
>Tha's fine, tha's fine. You're in
>Charge here, for the time bein'. They're
>Simple men you've got followin' you, but
>They all want to live. They won't be
>Followin' Bill Anderson or anybody who's
>Only int'rested in dyin'. We can't
>Kill Feds if we're dead.

QUANTRILL:
>I can't believe that so many of the
>Men are ready to follow him to their
>Deaths. They may want to live,
>But they'd follow Anderson if he led them.
>Why do we bother
>Running and
>Hiding if it's all going to end
>In some blind raid that'll kill us all?
>The guerillas' purpose is to
>Kill,
>Not be killed. You're right;
>We can't kill if we're dead.
>Neither can I lead if there's
>No one left to lead. Of course,
>That may be idle worry. Between
>You and Anderson, a knife or bullet is
>Bound to find its way to my heart.

TODD:
>I guarantee you this: if Bill
>Anderson kills you,
>It'll be his death too.

>>TODD *smiles. He and* QUANTRILL *exit. Blackout.*

SCENE SEVEN

Spotlight on JESSE.

JESSE: Now, George Todd had been the Colonel's right-hand man all along, so it came as no surprise to the others when he jus' kinda started sharin' command. Todd seemed to live a charmed life; he'd lead his men into a fight, make himself a prime target, an' always come out alive . . . even when the rest o' his men didn't. All the boys were sayin' Todd'd take command if anythin' ever happened to the Colonel. So, the time arrived when George Todd an' Bill Anderson decided they was ready to challenge Quantrill's power . . .

Spotlight is extinguished as the stage lights come up, revealing a campfire scene. QUANTRILL *is in a central position, flanked or surrounded by* FRANK, TODD, *and* ANDERSON.

QUANTRILL:
    The time has come for me to decide on
    My second-in-command. We number well
    Over a hundred, and we need to split up
    In order to function freely.

ANDERSON:
    Always talk. It don't make any
    Diff'rence. The men know who they
    Follow.

QUANTRILL:
    Tell me, Anderson, if you were in
    Command, just how would you propose to
    Fight the Federal troops?

ANDERSON:
>   Ride right down their throats, screamin'
>   An' shootin'. Plow right through 'em like a
>   Knife through butter.

QUANTRILL:
>   That settles it. I want the men to be
>   Led, not
>   Butchered. George Todd is
>   Second-in-command.

ANDERSON:
>   Todd! Always Todd! If he wasn't so damn
>   Lucky he'd have been dead months ago. The first
>   Time he leads a charge he'll be shot out of
>   His saddle.

TODD:
>   Save it, Bill. Since the Colonel has
>   Chose me to be his second, I got a
>   Plan to suggest. Tonight we ride to
>   The border an' burn a few Kansas
>   Farms an' farmers.

QUANTRILL:
>   That's foolish, Todd. We'll stay here for
>   A few more days, send out scouts to see
>   Where the closest Federal troops are at.
>   That sounds like one of Anderson's
>   Crazy plans.

ANDERSON has pulled a gun and holds it to QUANTRILL's head, whom he has come up behind secretly.

ANDERSON:
>   It is, Colonel.

He slowly clicks the gun's hammer.

>   Any other kind words for "Bloody" Bill an'
>   His crazy plans? You wanna tell me again

How stupid I am, an' how I'm gonna get me an'
All my men killed?

TODD:
Put the gun away, Bill.

ANDERSON:
Sure, George. Just talkin' to the
Colonel.

TODD:
Well, I'll do the talkin' now. Colonel
Quantrill, it seems that the men've been
Talkin' 'bout you behind your back. Yes,
Sir, they say they think you're through.
Know why? They say you've turned yella. They're
Sayin' that's why we been holed up here
For a month.

QUANTRILL:
You're a bigger ass than Anderson.
I'm afraid of no man. You, Todd,
You don't scare me. Or Anderson.
Both of you like to talk tough.
You don't scare me.

TODD: *(Advancing upon* QUANTRILL *like a madman)*
Is that right! I don't scare you,
Colonel? How about this?

He draws his pistol and holds it in QUANTRILL's *face.*

Are you scared of me, now? 'Fraid?
Huh? Say it.
This ain't a whiskey bottle I'm wavin'
Now. Say it.
You're 'fraid of me.
You hear me? Say it!
Say it or I'll blow your head off!

QUANTRILL, *downcast, mutters inaudibly.*

>
> Louder! Louder! So the
> Whole camp can hear you.

QUANTRILL: *(Slowly)*
> I'm
> Afraid of you.

ANDERSON *and* TODD *laugh loudly.* FRANK *joins in uncertain laughter.* QUANTRILL *quietly turns and exits offstage.*

TODD: *(Yelling after* QUANTRILL*)*
> Don't run so fast, Colonel, you'll
> Catch cold!
> Frank, go spread the news that
> Colonel Quantrill's gone on
> Perm'nent leave.
> Tell 'em we're now called
> "Todd's Gang."

ANDERSON:
> An' tell 'em we ride tomorrow.

FRANK *exits.*

> Say, Bill, you ever been offered a
> Second-in-command? I think it
> Might be arranged.

TODD *and* ANDERSON *walk offstage together, laughing and talking. Blackout.*

SCENE EIGHT

Spotlight on JESSE.

JESSE: When Colonel Quantrill left, there was only a few that left with him. George Todd became leader o' all three divisions o' Quantrill's troops. Wasn't long 'fore he an' Bill Anderson had a partin' o' the ways, though, with several o' the boys leavin' to ride with "Bloody" Bill, includin' myself. More an' more, the names George Todd an' Bill Anderson were talked 'bout, while nobody said much 'bout Colonel Bill Quantrill. Well, the day o' reckonin' had to come. After leadin' his men into so many battles an' never sufferin' so much as a wound, one day George Todd was sittin' on his horse on top o' a rise when somebody jus' put a bullet in his neck. Killed 'im without a fight. Then it wasn't but a few days later, I had to find the Colonel to give 'im an import'nt message. You have to 'scuse me. I—I've gotta go now. *(Looks up at spotlight)* Now you can turn it off. *(Waving it away)* Off, son. You deaf?

Spotlight fades out as JESSE *rises from his seat and runs upstage to where* QUANTRILL *is sitting on a rock.*

Colonel Quantrill! Colonel! They've
Killed Bill Anderson.
QUANTRILL: *(Looking up blankly)*
Killed him? Who? His men?
JESSE:
No, the Feds.
QUANTRILL: *(Standing up)*
So I *do* win. Even after they ordered him to
Try to get me.
Tell me what happened.

JESSE:
> Happened near Orrick. He was leadin' the company,
> Scoutin', sorta, when the Feds led 'im
> Into an ambush. Bill knew it was an ambush,
> But he rode right into it. We was far enough behind 'im,
> We got away. But they filled ole Bill fulla
> Lead an' then they took his body.

QUANTRILL:
> Where did they bury him?

JESSE:
> Bury 'im! They cut off his head an'
> Dragged his body through the streets.
> If that wasn't enough, then they hung his
> Head 'top of a telegraph pole.

QUANTRILL: *(Slight chuckle)*
> Sounds kind of "barbaric" to me.
> So, Bill Anderson, even blood lust dies. The
> Charmed life lasts only so long;
> The fate that sustains us suddenly
> Retires. Fate is a strange lady, young
> Jesse James. She allows us to ride into
> Lawrence with thousands of Unionists
> Nearby, slaughter and rob an entire
> Town, then ride back to our own
> Country with almost no losses. Then
> When we least expect it, George Todd or
> Someone like him takes a bullet in the
> Neck. Or Bill Anderson gets what's been
> Coming to him for years.

JESSE:
> Guess you've been pretty
> Lucky, Colonel. You're still kickin'.

QUANTRILL:
> I've been lucky, true, but I've
> Also been careful. Careful not to
> Depend on anyone but Bill Quantrill.
> Careful not to listen to anyone

But Bill Quantrill.
Did you know I used to be a
Schoolteacher? Farm children, mostly.
The most important thing I could teach
Them was not to depend on others. Nothing
Is more important. Even glory takes
Second place. Names like Bill Anderson,
George Todd,
Cole Younger, even
Jesse James,
Will they outlast that of Quantrill?
Which names will history choose
To keep
And which discard?

JESSE:
It ain't the names that are import'nt,
Colonel. It's how many times you win
Or lose that makes other men
'Member you.

QUANTRILL:
You're too young to be a romanticist,
Jesse James. That kind of thinking is
Reserved for men who can
No longer command, for old men and weaklings.
The bravery in battle gives infamy,
But not immortality. It's names, not
Deeds, that will outlive us.

He looks away from JESSE, *no longer addressing him.*

All the blood I've spilled, all the
Lives I've ended, what do they count
Against one hour of life after I'm
Dead? Can they buy me immortality?

JESSE *hangs his head, shakes it, and slowly walks offstage. His spotlight now comes on, centers on* QUANTRILL, *while all other lights on stage are extinguished.*

Did it save Todd? Or Anderson? Do
They listen now to the dying screams
Of the men they killed? Do their men
Still follow them in death? This I
Cannot bear, that after death those
Who have led in life should be
Punished by becoming
The followers, while those who filled the
Bottommost ranks, those who were cowardly,
Should take up the charge from the front,
And for all eternity we shall be led into
Suicide raids, hopeless ambushes, certain
Slaughter, and die again a
Thousands times over.
Black flags, oaths, nothing will prevail
When death finally arrives. Yet, are there
Any alternatives? If the war ended today,
Would I simply go back to teaching school?
I could not.
I've seen too much of life through death.
Besides, how many of the little faces
Would reflect the faces of men I've
Shot down? How many orphans by the hands of
Quantrill and the bushwhackers?
Long past is the opportunity to
Change my destiny. I am a rebel leader, and
I shall die one.
If only I knew the time, then I would not
Battle with fate. I would make my
Surrender to death, knowing full well that,
Like Quantrill,
He never takes prisoners.
Neither does he lose. His greatest
Allies are military leaders. His most
Coveted prizes, the same.
He is the

Supreme commander, the awe-inspiring
Champion of every battle ever fought. What
Chance have I against that kind of leader?
Death, I
Salute you.

With a mock salute and smile, QUANTRILL, *weary, walks offstage, the spotlight trailing slowly after. Blackout.*

Curtain.

NATIONAL PARK

Characters

BOOTHE, a Democrat
LENNAN, an anarchist
SACKO and VAN ZEDDI, Fascists
DILLEN, a Republican
AMEALIA, a Whig
OTTO BAHN, a Socialist

BOOTHE is an actor, arrogant, witty and melodramatic; LENNAN is an old man, trench-coated, bearded, revolutionary; SACKO and VAN ZEDDI are adults in children's clothing, who speak in fragmented phrases except when they are alone; DILLEN is an officer of the law, whose accent is decidedly "Dylanesque"; AMEALIA is an elderly lady, prim, stoic, and disinterested; OTTO BAHN is a dedicated bird-watcher, his eyes constantly glued to his binoculars.

Scene: The stage is decorated as a park. There is a park bench located downstage center. Upstage and to the right of it, there is a monument of some sort. The sounds of birds chirping are heard throughout the play, with assorted other "park" noises being thrown in occasionally as well.

OTTO BAHN *walks onto stage, and for the duration of the play walks around staring into the trees through his binoculars. He is oblivious to other characters.* AMEALIA *is sitting at one end of the park bench, looking straight ahead, paying attention to no one.* BOOTHE *enters, appearing lost or confused. He looks around himself, frequently appearing as though he has forgotten where he is.*

BOOTHE: I rarely play a town that has more than one theatre. There is usually one meeting hall . . . one theatre, or what-have-you, and it would be difficult to confuse it with anything else. . . . If one is in doubt, one can always walk up to someone and ask, "What theatre is Mr. Boothe playing tonight?" *(Sarcastic)* Everyone is more than happy to oblige.

LENNAN *enters from stage left during* BOOTHE's *speech, unaware of* BOOTHE's *presence. He is intently studying a small notebook and periodically pauses to write in it. He walks downstage and sits on the park bench at the end opposite* AMEALIA.

LENNAN: ". . . In every country, stir up hatred of your own government. This is the only work worthy of an anarchist."
BOOTHE: *(Noticing* LENNAN*)* Ah, here is a citizen of, doubtless, stable and helpful nature.

LENNAN: "The bomb is God, the knife is the Father, and the gun, the Holy Ghost."

BOOTHE: *(Approaches park bench and clears his throat)* Uh-hum.

No response from LENNAN.

My good sir.

LENNAN *absently looks up.*

What theatre is Mr. Boothe playing tonight?

LENNAN: Theatre?

BOOTHE: Or meeting hall.

LENNAN: There's to be a meeting?

BOOTHE: Not a meeting, no, a play.

LENNAN: Whose play?

BOOTHE: Mr. Boothe and his company.

LENNAN: *(Disinterested, bows and returns to his notebook)* Very nice.

BOOTHE: *(Momentarily abashed. He looks around as though for an answer)* My question?

LENNAN: *(Does not look up)* Is?

BOOTHE: *(Impatiently)* What theatre is Mr. Boothe playing tonight?

LENNAN: How should I know? Don't bother me. Why don't you ask your questions of Mr. Boothe?

BOOTHE: *(Smiling)* Impossible.

LENNAN: *(Closing his notebook, exasperated)* What do you mean, impossible?

BOOTHE: I, sir, am Boothe the actor.

LENNAN: *(Bows, reopening his notebook, muttering under his breath)* Bourgeois lunatic.

BOOTHE: Do not be ashamed, sir, many of my most ardent admirers do not recognize me once I leave the stage. *(Turns his back to* LENNAN *and begins pacing, motioning)* But then, how is that possible? After all, did not the great bard himself say the whole world's a stage?

LENNAN: *(Once again absorbed in the notebook)* "When they give you arms . . . take them. Only the conquest of political power through destruction of the government by the proletariat can insure peace!"
BOOTHE: Aye, the world's a stage, and every clod a prop. *(Bends to pick up a rock)* Alas, poor stone, I knew thee not.

BOOTHE *tosses the rock over his shoulder. It hits the bench with a loud clunk, the jolt making* LENNAN *jump up and stare wildly for a moment before focusing on* BOOTHE.

LENNAN: "When they give you arms . . . take them!"

LENNAN *throws the rock at* BOOTHE *and hits him in the back.* BOOTHE *cries out and falls to the floor. He lies motionless as* SACKO *and* VAN ZEDDI *come running in.*

SACKO: What—
VAN ZEDDI: —have—
SACKO: —you—
VAN ZEDDI: —done?
LENNAN: Done? What have I done? I have merely struck another blow for the movement. Another pest to the proletariat . . . kaput!
SACKO: *(Muttering under his breath)* Crazy—
VAN ZEDDI: —anarchist—
SACKO: —nut.
BOOTHE: *(Jumps to his feet)* My good fellows, the truly talented actor is invincible.

LENNAN *shakes his head sadly and again studies the notebook.* BOOTHE *gestures skyward.*

Thinkst thou to quell me? Nay, cretin! *(He looks at* SACKO *and* VAN ZEDDI *tenderly)* Boys, boys, maybe you can help. Tell me, what theatre is Mr. Boothe playing tonight?
SACKO: Who—
VAN ZEDDI: —is—

SACKO: —Mr.—
VAN ZEDDI: —Boothe?
BOOTHE: Of course, I am referring to Mr. Boothe, the famous actor.
SACKO: Actor?
BOOTHE: Yes, you know, star of the stage, baron of the boards, titan of the theatre.
VAN ZEDDI: Theatre?

SACKO *and* VAN ZEDDI *look at each other, scratching their heads.*

BOOTHE: *(Gesturing, a la charades)* Playhouse.
SACKO: Is it—
VAN ZEDDI: —bigger—
SACKO: —than a—
VAN ZEDDI: —bread—
SACKO: —box?
BOOTHE: *(Nodding vigorously)* Much, much.

LENNAN *has risen from the bench and is pacing, moving his lips as he reads from the notebook, occasionally mumbling audibly.*

SACKO: Animal—
VAN ZEDDI: —vegetable—
SACKO: —or mineral?

BOOTHE *shrugs and puts his hand to his chin. He is completely stymied by the question.* SACKO *and* VAN ZEDDI *begin playing leapfrog.*

LENNAN: *(Stops pacing and turns to face the audience; reading)* "Who provides the backbone of industry? Is it the rich? The advantaged? The privileged? No, it is the sad earth beneath the shoes of the rich, the proletariat, the ashes from the fire." *(Emphatically spits)*
BOOTHE: *(Claps and whistles)* Here, here! Well performed!

LENNAN *sneers at* BOOTHE, *as* SACKO *and* VAN ZEDDI *come running up to him.*

SACKO: *(Touches* LENNAN*)* Tag—
VAN ZEDDI: —you're—
SACKO: —it!
LENNAN: I'm . . . it?
VAN ZEDDI: Yes—
SACKO: —you're—
VAN ZEDDI: —it!
BOOTHE: Then there's no doubt about it. He's it. Oh, woe, what can one do when no longer it? Is there life after it? Can we reach the great it in the sky? Is it *it? (Shrugging)* Oh, well, that's it. But there's always . . . new parts, new starts, *(Starts swaying and works into a soft-shoe)*
    new lights, new plays, new nights, new days,
    new towns, new faces, new sounds, new places,
    new heights, new shoes, new sights, new news!

He finishes with a flourish on one knee. SACKO *and* VAN ZEDDI *cheer and clap.*

Ah, back in the spotlight again.

LENNAN *has returned to the bench and is again studying the notebook. He reaches into a small sack beside him, withdrawing a small bottle of wine and a hard roll.*

LENNAN: Yes, yes. Even a revolutionary must have nourishment.

SACKO *and* VAN ZEDDI *slowly walk to one side of* LENNAN, *watching him eat. They talk softly, in complete sentences.*

SACKO: Can you see clearly?
VAN ZEDDI: Quite clearly, thank you.
SACKO: What is that he's eating?
VAN ZEDDI: It's a gopher.

SACKO: A gopher?
VAN ZEDDI: Yes, I'm quite sure of it. Gophers are brown, aren't they?
SACKO: Yes, they are.
VAN ZEDDI: And that thing he's eating. It's brown, isn't it?
SACKO: Yes, it is.
VAN ZEDDI: Then it's settled. He's eating a gopher.
SACKO: What about the bottle?
VAN ZEDDI: What about it?
SACKO: What's he got in it?
VAN ZEDDI: I don't have any idea.

BOOTHE *has been watching from a distance and now approaches till he stands directly behind* SACKO *and* VAN ZEDDI.

BOOTHE: Well, what's the word, boys?

SACKO *and* VAN ZEDDI *both jump, and answer rapidly.*

SACKO: We're—
VAN ZEDDI: —only—
SACKO: —watching—
VAN ZEDDI: —sir.
BOOTHE: Yes, of course. Well, what's the old codger up to?
SACKO: He's—
VAN ZEDDI: —eating—
SACKO: —a gopher—
VAN ZEDDI: —but we—
SACKO: —can't tell—
VAN ZEDDI: —what—
SACKO: —he's drinking.
BOOTHE: Eating a gopher? But you don't know what's in the bottle? *(Winks)* Well, we'll have an answer to that question soon enough! *(Straightens himself, takes a deep breath, walks stiffly toward* LENNAN, *grabs the bottle of wine, and speaks rapidly)* Food Inspector Number Three-Zero-Five, testing beverages for safe level of sanitary contamination. To your

health. *(Quickly chugs the bottle)* No doubt about it, a bad year. You have my condolences.

BOOTHE *hands the bottle back to* LENNAN, *who in turn throws it while* BOOTHE *ducks, the bottle missing him and flying offstage.*

SACKO: *(As* BOOTHE *returns to them)* Well—
VAN ZEDDI: —what—
SACKO: —was—
VAN ZEDDI: —it?
BOOTHE: Well, boys, the plain truth of the matter is, it was *(Falls to the ground, writhes, then lies motionless)* arsenic.
SACKO: *(Softly, so as not to be heard)* Let's go sample the old man's gopher.

VAN ZEDDI *nods and the two split up, each approaching the bench from a different side.*

SACKO: *(Yelling)* STRIKE!

SACKO *raises a fist in the air, and* LENNAN *lays down his roll, to mimic him, smiling.* VAN ZEDDI *quickly picks the roll up, takes a bite from it, and replaces it.*

LENNAN: What a fine youngster you are.

LENNAN *puts down his arm, picks up his roll and nibbles on it.*

VAN ZEDDI: *(Yelling)* STRIKE!

He raises his fist and repeats the earlier business, with LENNAN *following, while* SACKO *samples the roll.*

LENNAN: Not to be outdone by your sharp young friend, eh?

He chuckles to himself, adding "Fine lads, fine lads," while picking up the notebook and munching the roll. SACKO *and* VAN

ZEDDI *run off together, whisper briefly, then return and stand in front of* LENNAN. *He gradually notices them and raises his fist.*

STRIKE!

He holds his fist up for several seconds, until he sees the two are not going to join him.

Why, what's the matter?
SACKO: —Sir—
VAN ZEDDI: —there is—
SACKO: —something—
VAN ZEDDI: —wrong—
SACKO: —with—
VAN ZEDDI: —your—
SACKO: —gopher.
LENNAN: My what?
SACKO: Your—
VAN ZEDDI: —gopher. It—
SACKO: —tastes—
VAN ZEDDI: —like an—
SACKO: —old—
VAN ZEDDI: —bread roll.
BOOTHE: *(Rises)* Things are not what they seem, my friends. The phoenix rises from the ashes.
LENNAN: *(Ignores* BOOTHE*)* What are you talking about? What do you mean, my gopher tastes like an old bread roll? I don't have a gopher.
SACKO: No—
VAN ZEDDI: —gopher?
BOOTHE: *(Rushing over)* No, boys, not everyone is so lucky. No, I had a gopher once.
SACKO: You—
VAN ZEDDI: —did?
BOOTHE: *(Singing, possibly to the tune of "I'm Looking Over a Four-Leaf Clover")*
  Oh, I had a gopher,

A fine one named Rover;
I taught him to bring me my tea;
Till one day he dropped it,
Resultantly slopped it,
And I stuffed him to hang on my tree.

LENNAN: *(Clapping his hands over his ears)* Enough! *(Stands up and walks away from the bench, notebook in hand, shaking in anger)* Capitalist lunatic.

BOOTHE: What did you think of that, boys?

SACKO: Oh, sir—

VAN ZEDDI: —would you—

SACKO: —stuff us—

VAN ZEDDI: —a gopher—

SACKO: —too?

BOOTHE: *(Smiling, but shaking his head)* Sorry, boys, but I retired from that game years ago.

LENNAN: *(Reads from where he is standing)* "The threats to the future of the proletariat must be purged. Death is the only purgation. It is the final purgation." *(He eyes* BOOTHE *carefully)* Threats. Purged. Death.

LENNAN *reaches into the bag that held his lunch and pulls out a gun equipped with a silencer. This he quickly stuffs into a pocket of his trench coat.*

SACKO: Well—

VAN ZEDDI: —I guess—

SACKO: —we'll just—

VAN ZEDDI: —have to—

SACKO: —find—

VAN ZEDDI: —and stuff—

SACKO: —a gopher—

VAN ZEDDI: —ourselves.

BOOTHE: It's the only way.

SACKO *and* VAN ZEDDI *link arms and walk over to wherever* OTTO BAHN *is at. They stand behind him for a moment, aping his actions by holding their fists to their eyes and looking skyward.*

SACKO: *(Tapping* OTTO BAHN *on the shoulder)* Please—
VAN ZEDDI: —sir—
SACKO: —could you—
VAN ZEDDI: —help us—
SACKO: —find—
VAN ZEDDI: —a gopher?

OTTO BAHN *does not take his eyes from the binoculars, but takes one hand and motions "shoo" to* SACKO *and* VAN ZEDDI. *They retreat out of earshot and again speak in complete sentences.*

SACKO: What a stuffed shirt.
VAN ZEDDI: A selfish pig.
SACKO: Bloated toad.
VAN ZEDDI: Swelled head.
SACKO: Inflated ego.
VAN ZEDDI: Indignant clod.
SACKO: Inflamed toenail.
VAN ZEDDI: Repulsive lizard.
SACKO: Arrogant S.O.B.

VAN ZEDDI *smiles and shakes* SACKO's *hand vigorously. During* SACKO *and* VAN ZEDDI's *interaction with* OTTO BAHN, BOOTHE *has been rehearsing his lines for the evening performance, mumbling, walking through blocking, etc.* LENNAN *has been stalking him, his hand in the pocket containing the silenced gun.*

BOOTHE: *(Walking over to* AMEALIA; *facing her in front of the bench)* Excuse me, gracious madame, but you appear to be a patron of the arts.

No reaction from AMEALIA.

The state of affairs being thus, perhaps you could enlighten me upon a certain topic that is very close to home.

Still no reaction from AMEALIA.

The topic is this: what theatre is Mr. Boothe playing this evening?

LENNAN: *(Standing behind* BOOTHE, *his hand in the gun pocket thrust forward)* Death liberates all!

At this moment, BOOTHE *bends down and picks a flower which is beside his left foot. As he does so, there is a loud "click" and* AMEALIA *slumps over on the bench.*

BOOTHE: *(Straightening up)* For you, madame—*(Smiles)* Naptime, eh?

LENNAN *hurries away; exits offstage.*

Well, a little token to enhance your fancies, my lady. *(He tucks the flower into* AMEALIA's *hair)* May your dreams give you wings and fly you to heaven.

SACKO *and* VAN ZEDDI *approach* BOOTHE *from where they stood talking.*

SACKO: Sir—
VAN ZEDDI: —we want—
SACKO: —to hunt—
VAN ZEDDI: —a gopher.
SACKO: Could—
VAN ZEDDI: —you—
SACKO: —help—
VAN ZEDDI: —us?
BOOTHE: Now, didn't I tell you boys that I retired from all that? Gophering? I'm too old for gophering now. I'm no longer into gophering. The theatre has taken its place. The theatre is my—goddess.
SACKO: Goddesses?
VAN ZEDDI: Gophers?
SACKO: What's—
VAN ZEDDI: —the—

SACKO: —difference?
BOOTHE: *(Winking)* It's all in the spelling, boys.

SACKO and VAN ZEDDI look at each other, thoroughly puzzled. Meanwhile, BOOTHE begins some kind of quasi-Fred-Astaire dance and falls in behind OTTO BAHN, mimicking him as SACKO and VAN ZEDDI did. SACKO and VAN ZEDDI sit down on the bench, shoving the body of AMEALIA aside to make room, and LENNAN reenters from stage left, again stalking BOOTHE. BOOTHE does not notice him as he approaches. BOOTHE sings as he dances.

> Let's all sing like the birdies sing,
> Tweet, tweet-tweet, tweet-tweet.

LENNAN: *(Standing in back of the dancing BOOTHE, he thrusts the gun pocket forward)* Workers of the world, unite!

On LENNAN's last word, BOOTHE slips and falls down. There is a loud "click," and OTTO BAHN also falls to the ground. SACKO and VAN ZEDDI come running over to help BOOTHE up. LENNAN hurries away, starts to sit at the bench, sees AMEALIA, and backs away.

SACKO: Oh—
VAN ZEDDI: —sir—
SACKO: —are you—
VAN ZEDDI: —all right?
BOOTHE: *(Stands up, shaking the dust off)* I'm fine, boys, just a miscue. *(Looks at his watch)* My, my, it is getting late. I've just got to find someone who can direct me to the theatre.

LENNAN, who has been backing off stage left, is met by DILLEN, who is entering.

DILLEN: Blowin' in the wind, friend?
LENNAN: Ah, I—a mistake, it was a mistake.
DILLEN: Tangled up in blue, true?
LENNAN: His fault. *(Frightened; pointing to BOOTHE)* That capitalist pig is to blame.

National Park

DILLEN *walks over to* BOOTHE, SACKO, *and* VAN ZEDDI, *with* LENNAN *in tow.*

DILLEN: *(To* BOOTHE*)* What's happenin', cap'n?
BOOTHE: Say, perhaps you can help me, officer.
DILLEN: Say the word, an' it's heard.
BOOTHE: Can you tell me what theatre Mr. Boothe is playing tonight?
DILLEN: *(Scratching his chin)* Mr. Boothe, Mr. Boothe. Oh, yeah, San Francisco group. They're headlinin' at the Poxy.
BOOTHE: *(Disheartened)* I was afraid you'd say something like that. Well, this being the state of affairs, I'll need a different kind of help.
DILLEN: *(Gesturing service)* Play, Mr. Tambourine Man.
BOOTHE: And what about you boys? Will you assist me, also?
SACKO: What—
VAN ZEDDI: —are we—
SACKO: —supposed—
VAN ZEDDI: —to do?
BOOTHE: Well, since I'm already late to rehearsal, I've simply got to run over one particularly troublesome scene right here. But I need everyone's help.

All nod enthusiastically, with exception of LENNAN, *who is jabbed by* DILLEN *and reluctantly nods.*

Good. Good. First of all, we need to position the old codger here.

BOOTHE *makes* LENNAN *sit at the base of the monument that is upstage from the bench.*

Next, you two boys will have to be flags.
SACKO: But—
VAN ZEDDI: —sir—
SACKO: —we've—
VAN ZEDDI: —never—
SACKO: —been—

VAN ZEDDI: —flags—
SACKO: —before.
BOOTHE: Tut, tut, it's really very simple.

He positions SACKO *upstage slightly from the monument.*

You will be the American flag.

He positions VAN ZEDDI *a few steps to the right.*

And you will be the Presidential flag. Any questions? Right. Now, officer, you—

SACKO *and* VAN ZEDDI *have begun flapping their arms loudly.*

Boys, boys, whatever are you doing?
SACKO: We—
VAN ZEDDI: —can't—
SACKO: —help it—
VAN ZEDDI: —sir, there's—
SACKO: —a strong—
VAN ZEDDI: —draft—
SACKO: —in here.
BOOTHE: *(Frowns; scratching his chin)* Touch of realism, eh? You boys ever done any character acting? *(Waves his arms)* Enough of this. Please, everyone, your attention! Now, officer, you are to be an officer of the law. You're a natural. I have a few lines to give. You'll be standing down here, near the Presidential flag. Got it? Okay. Now, when I start to run away after my lines, you yell, "Halt, assassin!" Now try that.
DILLEN: *(Clears his throat)* Halt, Walt.
BOOTHE: No, no, the line is—
DILLEN: *(Snaps his fingers rhythmically)* Whoa, Joe.
BOOTHE: No, it's—
DILLEN: Hey, Ray.
BOOTHE: No, no, no! It's "Halt, assassin!" "Halt, assassin!" "Halt, assassin!"

DILLEN: *(Looks around quickly)* Where?
BOOTHE: That's your line. Now repeat after me: "Halt, assassin!"
DILLEN: *(Shrugs)* Halt, assassin.
BOOTHE: Very good, very good. Really. Okay, ready now? Places, everyone!

He walks around to the back of the monument, behind LENNAN. *He climbs up onto the monument and is standing above* LENNAN *as he delivers his lines.*

Oh, this war, this bloody, bloody war. What cause is there for it? What illness so great that it cannot be cured? "If thy eye offendeth thee, pluck it out." You, sir, *(Pointing to* LENNAN*)* you are the cancer in the body of this great country. You are the ache in its heart of hearts.

SACKO *and* VAN ZEDDI *begin humming "America the Beautiful."*

What price, freedom? What price, happiness? What price, oh, what price is peace? Is the sacrifice too great?

DILLEN *also joins in, humming.*

Can any sacrifice be too great when the lives of countless thousands lie in the balance? Nay, when the stakes are so high, there can be no question of sacrifice. But how can one be worthy of such sacrifice? What is the ransom forfeited by these pounds of flesh? This is my answer to you, sir. *(Shapes his hand into a gun)* Sic temper—*(Pause)* sic temper—*(Pause. He has forgotten his line)* what the hell. Death to tyrants! Bang!

BOOTHE *leaps from the monument and lands between* SACKO *and* VAN ZEDDI. *They flap their hands violently.* BOOTHE *begins to run as* DILLEN *yells.*

DILLEN: Halt, assassin!

BOOTHE *continues running.*

Hey, halt, assassin!

BOOTHE *continues.*

HOLD ON, THERE! *(Pulls out a gun and fires it at* BOOTHE, *who falls near the front of the stage)*
LENNAN: *(Leaps up jubilantly, dropping his notebook)* The proletariat triumphs!

DILLEN *bends over and picks up the notebook, leafing through it. He stops at one page and frowns.*

DILLEN: Have a seat, Pete. *(Pushes* LENNAN *down)* Michael, we're gonna row your boat ashore. Takin' you downtown, clown.
SACKO: What's—
VAN ZEDDI: —wrong—
SACKO: —officer?
DILLEN:
> Dude's on his own,
> Has no direction home,
> He's a complete unknown,
> He's a rollin' stone.

DILLEN *leafs through notebook and comes back to the page he has marked.*

Check this: "And above all things, remember this: don't trust anyone under thirty."

SACKO *and* VAN ZEDDI *make "tsk-tsk" noises as* DILLEN *grabs* LENNAN *by the collar of his trench coat.*

I've got news for you, Lou. The word, nerd. You know what they say down at the station: "It's a hard,"

SACKO:
    It's a hard,
VAN ZEDDI:
    It's a hard,
SACKO:
    It's a hard,
DILLEN, SACKO and VAN ZEDDI:
    It's a hard rain soon will fall.

With LENNAN *in hand,* DILLEN *gives the "thumbs-up" sign to* SACKO *and* VAN ZEDDI, *and exits stage left.*

SACKO: So?
VAN ZEDDI: So what?
SACKO: So what do we do now?
VAN ZEDDI: For kicks, you mean?
SACKO: What else is there?
VAN ZEDDI: You're right. *(Pause)* I dunno. What you got in mind?
SACKO: You like to gamble?
VAN ZEDDI: Much as the next man.
SACKO: *(Looks at his watch)* It's almost five-thirty. Let's hit the subway station at a Hundred and fourth and try to go in through the exit doors.
VAN ZEDDI: Sure.

They pull cigars from their pockets, stick them in their mouths, and exit, skipping offstage.
Slowly, BOOTHE *raises his head and sees he is alone. He stands up, again brushing off the dust, and walks over to the body of* OTTO BAHN. *He kneels down slowly and tenderly raises the body up in his arms while kneeling.*

BOOTHE: Excuse me, sir, what theatre is Mr. Boothe playing tonight?

Curtain.

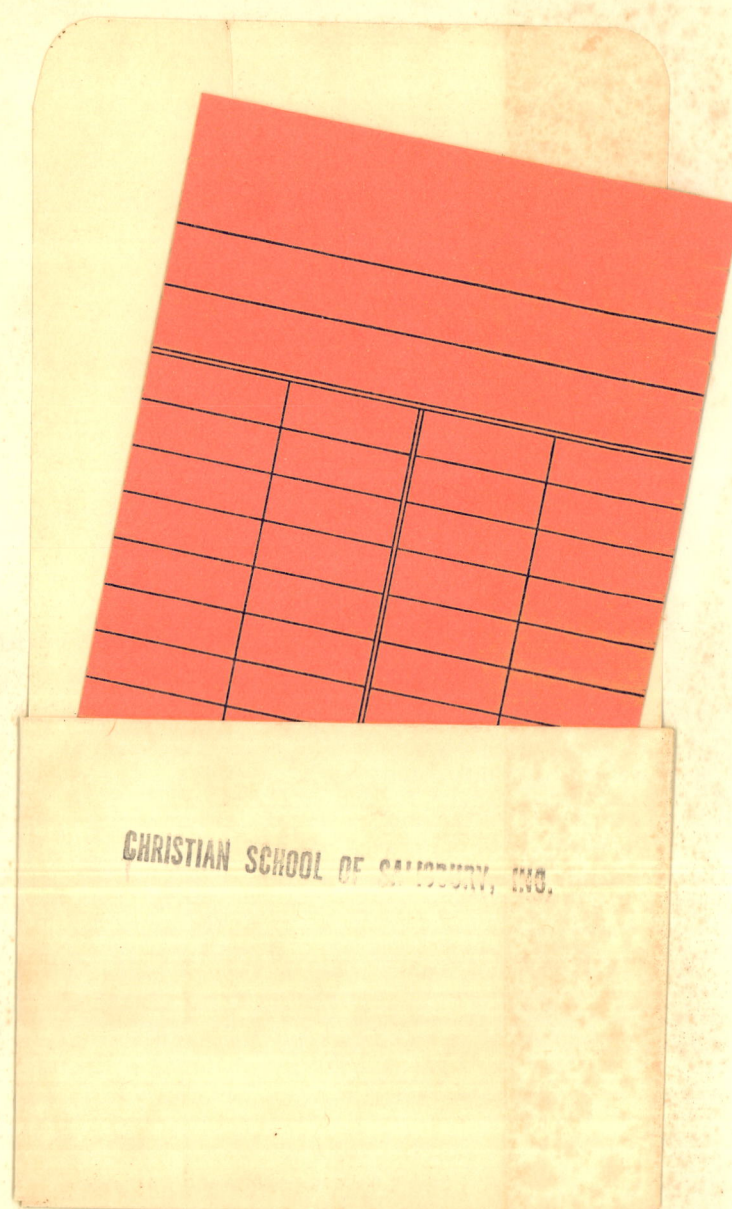